SOCIAL ETHICS
AND THE CHRISTIAN

SOCIAL ETHICS AND THE CHRISTIAN

Towards freedom in communion

ENDA McDONAGH

Professor of Moral Theology
St Patrick's College, Maynooth

MANCHESTER
UNIVERSITY PRESS

This book is based upon the
Ferguson Lectures delivered
in the University of Manchester
1978 by Professor Enda McDonagh

© Enda McDonagh 1979

Published 1979 by
Manchester University Press
Oxford Road
Manchester M13 9PL

ISBN 0 7190 0739 9

British Library Cataloguing in publication data

McDonagh, Enda
    Social ethics and the Christian.
    1. Christian ethics   2. Social ethics
    I. Title
    241   BJ1251
    ISBN 0–7190–0739–9

Typeset by Northern Phototypesetting Company, Bolton
Printed in Great Britain

CONTENTS

INTRODUCTION

When I was a doctorate student of theology in search of a dissertation some twenty years ago, I was advised by a prominent professor of moral theology that there was no really fundamental work to be done in moral theology and that I should confine my search to dogmatic and scriptural topics. The transformation of Roman Catholic moral theology in the intervening years has confounded that advice by being truly fundamental and it is still continuing. One of the more positive aspects of this development has been the convergence of the Roman Catholic and other Christian traditions. For a number of years I worked with an inter-church group seeking an ecumenical approach to ethics under the benign direction of Professor Gordon Dunstan at King's College, London. Some of the fruits of that work appeared in the volume which he edited under the title *Duty and Discernment* (SCM Press, 1975). Increasingly I found in reading, discussion, teaching and writing that denominational divisions seem to make little difference to basic approach to moral theology or Christian ethics. Neither the normative written sources of scripture, nor the significant theological reflections of Augustine or Aquinas, the Reformers or influential Catholic and Protestant contemporaries, offer any encouragement for denominational discrimination in ethics. The convergence in our time has been less a revolution than a restoration, albeit a restoration in the use of common resources to confront shared if fresh problems in a shared if changed and changing context. How far this convergence affects social ethics for Christians is discussed in the course of this book. It certainly provided a primary and positive reason for my particular choice of theme.

The negative reason for my choice was perhaps no less ecumenical. This was a growing conviction that no satisfactory, systematic and comprehensive social ethic had yet been achieved for contemporary Christians in any theological tradition. The absence seemed to me compounded by the frightening scale of the social moral problems faced by mankind today. More disturbingly still, personal ethics, which seemed so clear-cut and satisfactory in its basis and structure, if not always in its conclusions, appeared to be truncated and distorted by the lack of development of a social ethics or at any rate the satisfactory integration of the social and personal. What Christians needed was not a parallel elaboration of a social ethics but an integrated development of a personal-social ethics.

The sub-title, 'Towards freedom in communion', is intended to reflect both personal and social dimensions drawn together in a unitary fashion. The further principles elaborated such as 'through deeper differentiation to higher unity' are attempts to tease out the implications of such a personal-social ethics. The title and the book undoubtedly place the stress on the 'social'. This is partly in compensation for the neglect of the social in the past and a pointer to its necessary integration in the future. It also indicates the author's preference for what one might in other discourse term a 'field' rather than a 'particle' approach to ethics. It is in the social 'field' that the ethical aspect of the individual 'particle' is discovered, understood and given practical effect. The force and limitations of this analogy will, I hope, become clear in the course of the subsequent argument but its immediate impact should be a refocusing of our moral micro- or macro-scopes on the inter-relation and integration of particle and field, of person and community or society rather than on any isolated observation of either.

The most important word in the title and sub-title may be 'towards'. Although so much good Christian analysis has been done in both personal and social ethics, perhaps the time has come for a fresh bifocal approach. What is offered here is the beginning of a beginning. It moves from charting the needs and difficulties in chapter 1 to outlining a very general basis and structure in chapter 2. The generality is extremely important because the 'field' must be surveyed in all its breadth and depth. Yet it is also highly unsatisfactory because of its necessarily unfinished and imprecise condition. Some further precision is essayed in chapter three on social justice and human rights, while chapter 4 produces the most directly ethical-theological dialogue of the book in its confrontation of human society and kingdom of God.

This final confrontation really provides the substantive climax to the basic methodological approach of the whole work. Ethics, personal-social, is treated as primarily a human phenomenon which must be examined first of all on its own merits and then for the Christian confronted by the commitment and content of his faith. Such a method is not, I believe, false to such critical Christian sources

as the Covenant-Decalogue of Israel or the New
Testament teaching of which Romans 12-14 is a notable
example. As an explicitly developed method it has the
advantages of doing justice to morality and religion as
clearly distinguishable. It allows for moral dialogue
outside the Christian churches and promotes, I hope, a
deeper understanding of Christian faith and even of the
Christian God. In discussing personal morality I use, for
stylistic not sexist reasons, 'he' etc. throughout instead of
the more awkward 'he/she' etc.

The whole work, in method, basis, structure and
content, is marked by this 'towards' or – a key word in
the presentation – 'provisional' character. Not only has it
not arrived at clear and certain conclusions, it has at best
indicated some necessary starting points and some
fruitful directions. Perhaps other opportunities and other
moralists will clarify the starting points and make greater
progress in the right directions. For this opportunity this
author owes a special debt of gratitude to the University of
Manchester, its Faculty of Theology and, in particular,
Professor Ronald Preston and Professor Richard Hanson
for the invitation, encouragement and hospitality to
deliver the 1978 Ferguson Lectures. May this book prove
some modest return for their generosity.

While preparing the work I was fortunate to have been
given sabbatical leave by the Trustees of St Patrick's
College, Maynooth, to whom my thanks are also due. The
actual preparation began under the friendly roof of the
Dominicans at Blackfriars, Oxford. It was completed at
St Edmund's House, Cambridge, where I was
Leverhulme Visiting Fellow for 1978. To Blackfriars and
St Edmund's as well as to the Leverhulme Foundation I

am indeed indebted. In making and remaking sense of my script under very severe pressures my friends Maureen Valdez and Catherine KilBride who produced the typescript and so much more in patience and support are perhaps the most deserving of thanks.

Enda McDonagh
Saint Patrick's Day 1978

Chapter One

THE NEEDS AND THE DIFFICULTIES

The need for a social ethics

My choice of theme has been partly influenced by recent preoccupations as a lecturer in Moral Theology in the Roman Catholic tradition. After many years dealing with the basis of Christian morality as well as with particular areas of it, I came to some disturbing, if not exactly original, conclusions.

First of all, and perhaps rather obviously, despite an honourable tradition of what was called Catholic Social Doctrine[1] and a relatively sophisticated theological treatment of such major social problems as war,[2] there was no comprehensive and systematic body of reflection and analysis of the whole range of society's needs and problems in the light of Christian faith which one could call a Catholic/Christian social ethics or a social moral theology.[3] While not so familiar at that stage with other Christian traditions I at first suspected and later confirmed that they also were defective in this area.[4]

My second conclusion, while more tentative, was more disturbing in that it cast doubt over the whole enterprise of moral theology and Christian ethics as they had developed over the centuries. In reflecting on some of the more classical areas of so-called personal ethics such as respect for life, truth telling and sexual communication within the context of one-to-one relationships, I began to realise that an isolated personal or individual ethics was an abstraction derived from an abstraction, the one-to-one situation divorced from consideration of its social dimension.[5]

If I did not conclude from this immediately to the social as the essential starting point for all ethical reflection, and so the primacy of social ethics – Christian or humanist – I was forced to recognise the di-polarity of all ethical situations involving the two poles of person and society. Many examples of this are already recognised in practice, even if the requisite theoretical shift has not taken place. Abortion and euthanasia have obvious social as well as personal implications but the social are usually considered in an extrinsic fashion in terms of consequences, uncritically dominating or sub-ordinated to the personal need.

In some respects these are the pre-occupations of the theologian, the theoretician. Yet another important shift in his theorising on morality brought his head sharply out of the sand or at any rate up from his desk to consider the urgency of the social.

Moral theology and·Christian ethics have naturally regarded the Old and New Testaments, records of the Judaeo-Christian revelation, as the primary sources for their presentation of the morally good life for Christians. In the different traditions this had occurred in diverse ways, but biblical sources have usually provided both the starting point and ultimate reference point for consideration of Christian morality and Christian living.[6] This is not necessarily so, and there are a number of theologians today who deliberately as theologians adopt a different starting point for Christian reflection on moral questions. They prefer to begin with the data of human experience of morality, try to analyse and understand that and then confront it with their Christian faith.[7]

It would be foolish to ignore certain difficulties in this approach such as the apparently artificial dichotomy it introduces into the Christian's mind and life, particularly its separation between religion and morality. Some of these will emerge and be dealt with later; others I have enlarged upon elsewhere.[8] It would be more foolish to regard this as the only possible way of approaching ethics for Christians and thereby to jettison centuries of very important work by acute and committed Christian thinkers.

Its importance to me just now is not methodological but substantive. It is impossible to take as one's starting point the moral experience of one's time, indeed of one's own life, without acknowledging that the great moral problems of the day are in the most obvious sense social: questions of peace and war; of enormous affluence and abysmal poverty; of denial of basic rights; of torture, forced labour and arbitrary executions; of international terrorism; of discrimination because of race or sex or colour or age; of population growth; of industrial strife; of environmental pollution and diminishing natural resources. The list is endless. One might simply read out the headlines of any morning's paper to indicate the range and diversity to give some flesh and blood (mainly blood) to these skeletal categorisations. However, it hardly requires such concrete examples to underline how large groups and whole societies are affected by immense problems which can only be tackled by organised groups or societies. To expend one's intellectual resources exclusively on the nice distinctions involved in promise-keeping, or the not-so-nice involved in certain sexual practices, may be intellectually stimulating and even useful but it is back to head-in-the-sand moralising in the shadow of such towering social problems.

At some stage the moralist and particularly the Christian moralist, must, if he is serious about his avocation, attempt a systematic analysis of and some guidance for response to these major problems in what might be called a social ethics for Christians.

The difficulties

(a) Complexity of issues

The difficulties faced by the moralist are enormous. The number and diversity of the issues involved might seem to rule out any kind of overall approach which is not either superficial, banal and so useless; or else so comprehensive and inflexible as to result in a totalitarian prescription. How do you combine in the same system the problems of British Leyland with those of the Middle East or even those of discrimination based on race with those based on sex, or, to narrow the field still more to the economic and the local, the problems of inflation and rising costs of living with wage control and widespread unemployment?

And who would do the combining? What kind and range of expertise are we demanding of the poor moralist which would enable him to deal competently with international politics and diplomacy, the complexities of the economic order, the physical, biological, economic, legal and political dimensions of controlling pollution or of husbanding and fairly distributing natural resources?

(b) *The piecemeal approach*

In attempting to cope with this difficulty while escaping the trite generalisations about justice and peace or whatever, as well as the totalitarian prescriptions for a whole society, two strategies have been adopted.

The piecemeal strategy is self-explanatory. Ethical analysis of and prescriptions for questions of peace and war are developed independently of an ethics of economics and business which in turn are considered apart from that of use and abuse of environmental and natural resources. Separate ethical treatment is provided for industry, perhaps including strikes, perhaps not; for medical problems; for communications; for basic human rights; and all appear in article and book form and may even have a specialised journal.

Such a strategy has obvious advantages. It allows for detailed discussion of particular areas within which the moralist can attain some competence of his own at least to the point of being able to dialogue effectively with specialists in the field. These specialists in turn may be able to grasp and illuminate the relevant moral prescriptions more effectively than the moralist who must remain a partial outsider. They are also in a position to communicate the moral prescriptions more credibly to their colleagues and the wider public and they have closer association with whoever may ultimately implement these.

By allowing moralists to specialise in this way and so enabling them to co-operate with experts in various areas, a growing body of moral understanding of different and difficult social problems is gradually accumulated and communicated. We see many of the positive results of such a strategy in the work of Christian moralists throughout the world. And despite its limitations, which I shall discuss in a moment, this kind of work will always be necessary.

The limitations are serious. Each particular area is in its isolation self-distorting as well as distorting of the rest of society. To take one example: it is impossible to present a balanced and comprehensive view of medical ethics without taking into account the food, nutrition and hygienic needs of people, with implications for the distribution of resources and effect on the environment, with their implications for population growth, the structure of international trade or the standard of living of the affluent societies with their international and national political ramifications.

Taking a different line within the same area of medical ethics – the use and abuse of drugs goes far beyond any immediate code of prescription for the individual into the whole world of the drug industry, multinational corporations, animal and human experimentation, adequate testing and safeguards, fair and unfair advertising, provision of doctors and other medical personnel, the meaning of health, the significance of pain, quality of life, attitudes to the dying and to death. And these have all the further political and economic dimensions of which we are too well aware.

The difficulty of the piecemeal approach is not just that it is finally impossible to isolate a particular area from the whole pattern of society. This difficulty might be overcome jigsaw fashion by a sufficiently co-ordinated distribution of areas of specialisation with the specialists complementing each other's work to give an overall picture of a society's moral needs and required responses. This demands an act of faith in the skill and co-operation of both moralists and other specialists for which we have so far too little evidence. It might appear as a possible goal to be slowly approached if never finally reached.

The question, however, goes deeper. How the particular area is mapped and understood depends to a large extent on certain presuppositions of the moral map-maker. These presuppositions may and probably will be shared throughout a certain society or at least by that stratum of society from which the moralists and other specialists largely come. This will make the fitting together of the jigsaw that much easier but will be more likely to blind the co-operators to the role of their presuppositions in all their work and their need to examine and expose them.

Piecemeal moral surveying can proceed happily, indeed more happily, without such examination of the presuppositions, or, to change the metaphor, of the foundations on which the particular medical or economic structures rest. To examine the foundations is to call all the particular structures into question and possibly undermine the significance of various sectional moral analyses. To ignore the presuppositions or foundations is to run the risk of total moral misunderstanding and confine social ethics to a series of relatively trivial professional and possibly self-interested codes of behaviour.

(c) Ignoring morality in public issues

Facing such a dilemma the moralist, or the politician or economist, is tempted to confine his attention to the more

traditional fields of moral concern and equivalently de-
moralise whole areas of public and social behaviour. A
significant indicator of this is the House of Commons
tradition allowing a free vote on 'moral' issues, that is
issues affecting respect for life such as capital punishment,
abortion and euthanasia, and some sexual matters like
prostitution and pornography. A good recent example
was the Protection of Children Bill (against abuse for
pornographic purposes) debated on Friday 10 February
1978. The promoter of this Private Member's Bill claimed
on the BBC that evening that 'it was the first occasion a
moral issue had been debated in the House of Commons
for a long time'. So much for southern Africa and
Northern Ireland, for wages guidelines and blacklisting of
firms, for immigration and race relations, all discussed in
the Commons within the week.

Yet, it is important to understand what lies behind the
House of Commons convention and remarks of that kind.
The tradition of confining morality to personal relations
has been very influential in western society, not least
because of the attitude of the churches. Politicians are still
(dimly) aware that these wider issues have a moral aspect.
They tend to regard this as so obvious as to be not worth
mentioning, or as so abstruse and complex as to be not
worth the trouble seeking. In this they are not so far from
the position of many Christians – even church leaders and
moral theologians.

Two other contradictory forces are also at work. To
some extent all of us as citizens or politicians live off a
certain moral and religious capital which underlies
many of our moral attitudes and political decisions.
The most significant elements derive from the

theological/philosophical/moral regard for the value of the human person. Where some social practice or some proposed piece of legislation is clearly degrading of the human person our politicians and our social administrators are still by and large sensitive enough to oppose it. What constitutes 'inhuman and degrading treatment' may be easily obscured by self-interest, by the formidable difficulties raised by international terrorism and organised crime, or by the sheer complexity of certain problems of racialism or sexism.

Contradictory of all this moral and religious tradition, however, is the tradition of power and *realpolitik* which is associated fairly or unfairly with the name of Machiavelli. In this tradition moral considerations are bracketed out and whatever serves the interest of the government or the ruling group becomes the exclusive criterion of political or economic or industrial action. For propagandist reasons, to retain the support of the voter or the consumer or the general public, this will usually be disguised and may even be modified. Moral considerations do not play a role directly in this modification (or disguise) but they receive some indirect recognition from the power group as still effective and influential with the others. The great tyrannies of modern times under Stalin or Hitler or Idi Amin have sometimes felt the need for disguise in face of various people's moral sensibilities. Disguise is the final tribute of the amoral tradition in politics, economics and other power structures of the world to the continuing existence and influence of morality in social affairs.[9]

From issues to agents

The difficulties so far discussed have concentrated on the issues of which a moral analysis is necessary not for its own sake but in order that an adequate moral response may be made. The limitations of piecemeal analysis, the apparently insuperable difficulties of overall analysis, and the final inadequacy of the strategy of ignoring the moral dimensions of social problems in practice or in principle should be sufficiently discouraging to any moralist.

Further discouragement awaits him as he shifts the focus from the 'objective' moral demands revealed in the different areas to the *subjects* who must respond to these demands. These demands arising out of the needs of groups of people, sometimes very large groups, even whole countries and continents, can be met only by organised group response. The group, some group, is usually obliged to respond in an organised way to the needs of another group. The group in this sense becomes a moral subject, a centre of moral awareness and moral response. Such a concept of group as moral subject creates considerable conceptual difficulties. The moral consciousness of the group, its conscience, is difficult to define and almost impossible to form and locate. What do we mean by the conscience or moral consciousness of Britain or the Republic of Ireland in relation to the Northern Ireland question, to take a relatively confined example? How is this conscience recognised and located? Who is its keeper? How is it informed, formed, influenced? How does it arrive at its decisions? How does it implement them? How does it assess the moral value of its decisions subsequently? How does it repent of the

wrong ones? How make reparation for them, reform
them?

The first easy answer is to rule out these questions or at
least some of them such as repentance (and reparation?)
as mistaken in discussing social and political issues. This
reduces to removing the issues from moral consideration
altogether, which the previous discussion and our own
best traditions will not permit.

A more convincing easy answer would be to relegate all
responsibility and response in this issue at any rate to the
government of the day. The government must be the
keeper of the people's conscience in such matters and on
their behalf. For all its attractiveness, theoretical and
practical, this answer will not do, certainly not in the kind
of representative democracy we claim to cherish. It is the
people's conscience the government has to keep and on
the people's behalf it has to act. But what if it betrays that
conscience and acts immorally on the people's behalf? To
say that the government can be changed at the next
election will not protect the victims of its immoral
activities now. And where a bipartisan policy, formal or
informal, operates then change of government will not
lead to any change in this particular policy. Indeed,
despite the government-opposition tradition in our
democracies, we know full well that in issues where
national pride is at stake both sides are frequently too
blind to the issues involved, or too scared of appearing
unpatriotic and thus losing support, to admit past
mistakes and initiate new policies. As keepers of the
people's conscience and agents on their behalf they move
within very strict limits. The behaviour of the great
democracies – the United States of America, Britain,

France – as colonial or neocolonial powers bears eloquent testimony to this from Saigon to Calcutta to Algiers. The conscience of the people cannot be trusted unconditionally and uncritically to any government even for a fixed period of time without serious danger of betrayal.

The whole theory of representative democracy, of government by consent and under the law, resists such uncritical transference. The people retain their capacity to recognise, and freedom to act in face of, moral demands which the government ignores or resists or on which it is powerless to act. Important social changes in regard to slavery (ancient or modern, primitive or refined by the industrial revolution) to racialism and sexism, to torture and capital punishment, have been initiated without government support and sometimes against the whole weight of the establishment of which the government forms a part.

The conscience of the people has to be awakened by prophetic voices who understand more quickly and more deeply key social demands. It has to be informed through the media which can so quickly and powerfully, for good or ill, transmit information and ideas. This new awareness must be expressed in the organisation of the people to respond to the demand either through harnessing government resources where that is appropriate and possible, or through establishing effective voluntary organisations. A creditable amount of such moral awareness and response has been achieved in Britain and other countries by both governmental and voluntary agencies. Yet I have the uneasy feeling that such awareness and response may appear all too easy at the practical level while the conceptual difficulties about the group as moral subject have been made to appear irrelevant.

Despite the undoubted home achievements in welfare provision of all kinds for people of all races and ages and sexes, the distinctions within even this society of Britain are still powerfully rooted and frequently destructive. Differences of income, class, race, sex, nationality, educational and job opportunity have in the last decade been further unveiled as forms of that destructiveness. Any coherent moral awareness and response by the British people as a whole to their internal social problems remains uncertain and fragile. In relation to problems further afield, sometimes no further than Brussels or Belfast, the uncertainty and fragility are automatically increased. And when it comes to issues of war and starvation and human rights across the globe, even in areas where Britain has special ties such as India or to which it still has special responsibilities like Rhodesia, the coherence in awareness and response is scarcely discernible and deeply vulnerable

This is not a peculiar weakness of the British people or of the democratic system as I already indicated. Indeed, without any feeling of complacency it could be argued that both function as morally in these issues as the best. Practically, that best remains grossly inadequate. Theoretically, the basis of it is thoroughly confused. The relationship between theory and practice can never be finally and theoretically formulated, as will become increasingly evident. At this stage their mutual influence must be acknowledged and attempts made to promote a practice which is ethically responsible in the social field without adequate theoretical underpinning is doomed to eventual failure. In times of crisis, which are really times of decision, well-intentioned responses based on merely muddled awareness of the real moral issues, of the means of informing public conscience on them and of the structures of public responsibility in regard to them, will compound rather than resolve the crisis.

A Christian social ethics?

Granted that these social issues have a moral dimension and that the appropriate subject of moral response is the group or the people, with all the difficulties in terms of conscience or moral awareness and effective moral response which that invokes in theory and practice, why should there be a particular Christian aspect to all this? Is there, in other words, a specifically Christian social ethic or, at least, a specifically Christian demension to social ethics?[10]

As far as our discussion has gone so far the answer might seem to be: 'No, the issues themselves do not involve any specifically Christian doctrines.' Of course, the doctrine of creation or of a creator might seem to Christians on the one hand to root the demands in something of the absolute of the creator and on the other hand to provide a source of accountability in regard to the subjective obligations. Yet, Christians have, particularly in social issues, to work for and with peoples of various faiths and none. There is a *de facto* bracketing of the Christian dimension in analysing, communicating and responding to social moral problems. But is the bracketing necessary in theory? And could it be necessary in theory and irrelevant in practice? Do not the theoretical presentations by and for Christians basically ignore the bible on social morality while attaching great importance to it on questions of 'individual' morality? Are the doctrines of natural law or of the two kingdoms, which have tended to dominate Catholic and Protestant social ethics respectively, not really ways of leaving the biblical morality aside while fashioning, in ultimately non-Christian and indeed non-religious terms, an ethics for society that can be shared and, indeed, developed and influenced by non-Christians and non-theists?

It is doubtful if the invocation of the over-arching Christian virtue of love of neighbour is sufficient to make a hard and fast distinction between Christian and non-Christian social ethics. Whatever its origins, love of neighbour does not, in its immediate meaning or ultimate range, seem impervious to non-religious understanding or general acceptability. The fine distinctions made by some authors between *eros* and *agape*, between universal and altruistic love, or between benevolence and beneficence, do not seem to me to be well founded in the New Testament or finally defensible in psychological and moral analyses.

The difficulty of discovering and defending a specifically Christian social ethics has been compounded by the conviction of many moralists who are Christians of the impossibility of defending a specifically Christian ethics at all. For the most part, these moralists (and their critics) are concerned primarily with individual ethics but their arguments would apply *a fortiori* to 'social' ethics. While I retain my reservations about the individual-social distinction in ethics, I do not find the distinction relevant in refuting the arguments of those Christian theologians who deny that there is a specifically Christian ethics.

Admittedly, this denial is frequently qualified by confining it to a denial of a distinction in 'content' between Christian and secular or human ethics. (I do not think it irrelevant to this debate to ask: which secular or human ethics? But it is not necessary to pursue this point just here.)

Apart from content, a distinction in motivation (of the moral agent) is offered as a specifically Christian element. Where the motivation suggested is love of neighbour I do not see that the distinction is justified. Love of neighbour is, as I have said, capable of adequate non-religious interpretation. Where the agent is plural, as in social ethics, it is hard to argue to a non-reducible single motivation such as love of God or obedience to God's law or conformity to God's action in the world. For agents mixed religiously (and which social agents today are not?) the motivation will also be mixed. That way we cannot find a specifically Christian ethics.

I am doubtful whether the whole motivation debate has really contributed much to our understanding of the relationship between ethics and Christian faith. The sharp distinction which it suggests between the objectivity of the demands and the subjectivity of the responses, which may include religious motivation as a kind of overdrive, seems to me faulty psychologically and philosophically.

In the light of such considerations I will try to provide some outline of a social ethics for Christians, rather than a Christian social ethics. The general obligations, and their urgency, for the development and implementation of a

social ethics which Christians share with others, has
already been sufficiently indicated. The particular
relationship with Christian faith which such an ethics may
have will also be discussed in the subsequent chapters, as
we move from the basis and structure of a social ethics in
chapter 2, to the question of social justice and human
rights in chapter 3, and, finally, to the relationship
between Human Society and the Kingdom of God in
chapter 4. Central to the total argument will be the
understanding of human and Christian freedom as it
operates in and through community.[11]

Notes

1   This is officially expressed in a series of Papal Encyclicals the most
    important of which are the following: Leo XIII, *Rerum Novarum*
    (1891); Pius XI, *Quadragesimo Anno* (1931); John XXIII, *Mater et
    Magistra* (1961); John XXIII, *Pacem in Terris* (1963); Paul VI,
    Populorum Progressio (1967); Paul VI, *Octagesima Adveniens* (1971);
    Synod of Bishops, *Justice in the World* (1971). Compare Fremantle
    (ed.) *The Social Teachings of the Church* (Mentor-Omega Books, New
    York, 1963); Gremillon, Joseph, *The Gospel of Peace and Justice*
    (New York, 1975); Schooyans, Michel, 'Catholic social thought
    to 1966: an historical outline', *Church Alert*, 17, 1977 pp. 2–6.
2   Although he is not a Catholic, Paul Ramsey's treatment of the
    theology of the Just War provides the best contemporary
    treatment of a tradition initiated by Ambrose and Augustine,
    developed by Aquinas and reaching its climax in Francis de
    Vittoria. This is the tradition presented in the manuals of Catholic
    Moral Theology. Compare Ramsey, P., *War and the Christian
    Conscience* (Durham NC, 1961); Ramsey, P., *The Just War* (New
    York, 1968).
3   One of the most systematic available is Messner, J., *Social Ethics*
    (rev. ed., St Louis–London, 1965). However, like the works of
    Maritain or a contemporary essay such as Blanchette, A., *For a
    Fundamental Social Ethic* (New York, 1973), Messner remains in the
    philosophical idiom and does not tackle the strictly theological
    dimension.
4   The 'Protestant' approach which characterised the work of the

Christian Socialists of mid-nineteenth-century Britain, of the American Social Gospel, such commanding figures as Reinhold Niebuhr and later the World Council of Churches, is more clearly theological. However, it does not amount to a fully systematic presentation. Compare Grenholm, C. H., *Christian Social Ethics in a Revolutionary Age* (Uppsala, 1973). Dumas, A., 'The social thought of the World Council of Churches from 1925–1966', *Church Alert*, 17, 1977.

5   The recent approaches of existential and situation ethics were excellent examples of this but they were carrying on an age-old Christian tradition at least in their individualism.

6   Although, until recently, Roman Catholic moral theology was dominated by certain 'Natural Law' concepts, the overall extrinsic framework was of this biblical kind. More recent moralists such as Bernhard Haring have tried to make the biblical framework intrinsic to the morality.

7   Compare McDonagh, E., *Gift and Call* (Dublin, 1975).

8   See note 7 above.

9   A powerful current illustration of this is provided by Count Tolstoy in his book *Victims of Yalta* (London, 1978) on the behaviour of British politicians and public officials in regard to the repatriation of Russians against their will after World War II.

10   Compare Manaranche, A., *Y-a-t-il une ethique sociale chretienne?* (Paris, 1968). This useful work may in terms of my own approach be posing the wrong questions, as his work is more theological in its starting point and development.

11   On the theological question of freedom rather than social ethics compare Hodgson, P., *New Birth of Freedom* (Philadelphia, 1976) and the excellent book by Kurt Niederwimmer, *Der Begriff der Freiheit im Neûen Testament* (Berlin, 1966).

Chapter Two

THE METHOD, THE BASIS AND THE STRUCTURE

The method

It has been suggested that there are two basic methods of doing ethics and, in particular, doing social ethics for Christians: the natural law or primarily philosophical method, and the theological method.[1] Hitherto these two methods would have been attributed to the Catholic and Protestant traditions respectively.[2] In leaving aside this rather simple categorisation here I do not intend to belittle the achievements of these methods or traditions. In continuity with some previous work of my own,[3] but in what (I hope) is a corrective and development of it, I prefer to employ from the beginning a method which takes the interaction of Christian faith and ethics seriously but in a manner which distinguishes yet unites. The fuller meaning of the distinction in unity will emerge in the course of this and the following chapters.

The distinction provides the key to the primary analysis of social ethics as a human phenomenon, encountered as a human experience by each of us and shared by the Christian and non-Christian alike. Their accounts of and analysis of that experience may differ but they are open to intelligible dialogue on their respective positions or at any rate not precluded by the submergence of ethics in Christian faith. The distinction also enables the Christian to avoid a reduction of the Christian gospel to merely ethical considerations and categories, however universal and inspiring. The unity makes possible a synthesis within the Christian community and the individual Christian whereby Christian social living escapes a schizophrenic dichotomy.

Distinction or differentiation in unity goes not envisage side-by-side parallel existence of faith and ethics but a genuine interaction of a dialectical kind whereby mutual influence operates and higher unity is attained through deeper differentiation. This, as I hope to show, is not an artificial device introduced specifically to resolve difficulties in the relationship between faith and ethics but is an aspect of the structures of human experience and existence which is of particular significance in social ethics and in its relationship to our faith in the God of Jesus Christ.

Abiding by the distinction I will attempt first of all to discuss and analyse the basis and structure of social ethics as they emerge in human experience, at least my own, and then relate that to the basis and structure of Christian faith. In this way it may be possible to find at least a starting point for Christians in their understanding and application of a social ethics that will be sufficiently flexible and sensitive to the number, diversity and complexity of some of the social issues and social agents already discussed. At the same time it allows them to operate in genuine interaction and provisional integration with their Christian faith.

Provisionality

'Provisional' is another key word of the whole enterprise. My sub-title you may remember is 'Towards freedom in communion'. Again preserving the distinction it is possible to insist on the 'towards' character of both social ethics and Christian faith. This 'towards' character is reinforced in the case of social ethics by the continually changing nature of society and its needs. This applies in its own way to faith and our grasp of it. As 'towards' activities, both ethics and theological analysis issue in at least provisional achievements, genuine stages on the way, but open to revision and even radical trans-formation. The provisionality of our understanding of their distinction and unity is more fully revealed.

Provisionality rules out total comprehension and certitude. These do not belong within the human historical eon. But it does not rule out commitment or engagement with the best understanding we can attain and to the best moral response we can achieve. Provisionality is no more and no less a part of the condition of our human understanding and living than engagement and commitment are, as even the greatest lovers must in their reflective moments conclude.

The basis in human experience

The starting point and finally the basis for all analysis of human experience of morality (or more correctly the moral dimension of human experience) is the di-polar subject of person-in-community and community-of-persons to which I fleetingly referred in the first chapter.[4]

Let me explain more fully what I mean.

With the distinction between ethics and faith in mind I find it possible to recognise a moral dimension to human experience which manifests itself as obligation or call to behave in a certain way, or as ability to recognise a distinction between right and wrong or good and evil in my own and other people's behaviour. Probing this a little further I discover that this awareness and behaviour has been originally learnt from a community or series of communities (family, church, cultural and wider communities) and is internalised and personalised in a way that makes it more radically my own. Yet it is influenced by, expressive of and influences the varying relationships by which I am constituted a person-in-community.

All my 'personalised' actions (to borrow an americanism) are the 'personalising' of certain social as well as individual resources. And whether these actions are explicitly directed to a 'thou' in a one-to-one situation or are more widely intended for the plural 'we' or 'you' of society, they have social repercussions on the relationships by which I and thou, we and you, are tied into and in communication with that wider society. A community in turn responds morally out of its awareness and resources to the needs of particular groups or individuals within the community or to the needs of quite different communities by various formal and informal channels, but in doing so it affirms itself as a community-of-persons, a unity recognising the creative and irreducible differentiation of its individual members or persons. As the person is not reducible to membership of any particular group or community – like a pebble in a

pile of stones or more functionally an ant in an ant heap –
but retains his differentiated irreducible character, and so
may contribute creatively out of his difference to the
higher unity of the community. So the living community is
not reducible to the artificial and convenient alignment of
discrete individuals but depends for its living unity on the
creative interaction of increasingly differentiated
persons.[5]

Unity in differentiation, and a higher unity through
deeper differentiation, are at once the given and summons
of human society in the familial, ecclesial and civil,
regional and global contexts. Morally good social action
is action which promotes this higher unity through deeper
differentiation. It is to this that the moral subject or agent
as person or community is called. It is on the basis of the
gift and achievement of this that the subject responds.

Nature and biology

Person-in-community and community-of-persons need
to be concretely situated both in nature and in history.
The natural and biological dimensions of mankind
provide the immediate substrate for both person and
community/society (for the moment I will use these two
words interchangeably).[6] As continuous with nature, and
more specifically biological nature, mankind is part of the
animal kingdom. The individual human comes into
existence through the relationship or unity of two sexually
differentiated biological beings and is nurtured and grows
to maturity within some such relationship and
community. As a biological being his dependence on
others and their subsequent dependence on him – his

communal ties – are particularly marked. As a slow maturer, and in the biological sense a slow learner, relationships with fellow humans have to be enduring and deep. Crowning flower of the evolutionary tree he may be, but he is a particularly fragile flower and needs all the protection and support of his elders to survive at all, let alone thrive and develop.

Freedom and history

The biological unit and unity are not yet person and community in the proper sense. For that instinctive learning yields to intelligent and directed learning, instinctive caring to loving and directed caring, transforming natural bonds into moral ties. Freedom of movement becomes freedom of choice, decision and self-commitment. Evolution becomes history.

Human continuity with the natural and biological provides the basis for and is transformed by the discontinuity of human freedom and human history. The relationship is again dialectical and a further form of unity in differentiation for the human species and the human individual. As they emerge into history by the conscious discovery and exercise of their freedom they establish the distinctive traces of human personality and community in language and culture, morality and religion. By culture I mean man's adaptation of rather than to his environment, its further deliberate cultivation and creative transformation, the expression of his freedom.

Language and culture are as critical to the recognition and shaping of morality and religion as freedom is to their adoption and exercise. Freedom has always been taken for granted as essential for morality. But it has frequently been an impoverished idea of freedom of choice for the individual to do A or B while ignoring the communal context, the biological substrate and the temporal historical condition. It is only in this context, on this substrate and under this condition that true human freedom emerges, not simply as freedom of choice but the more mature freedom of decision, of engagement and commitment. Of such freedom history is made.

The making of history then is the moral challenge whose criterion is higher unity through the deeper differentiation. The personal growth, the fuller realisation or appropriation and utilisation of one's resources so that one becomes more truly oneself is the means whereby one achieves greater differentiation. Fuller appropriation of one's resources means greater capacity for self-disposition in decision and engagement, i.e. greater freedom. At the same time one enriches the community and enhances its unity by the possibility and actualisation of deeper bonds. The more fully differentiated and freed or liberated self has more to offer in relationship and so to unity. It is in relationship and so in unity that the greater differentiation may be achieved.

Let me illustrate this by a couple of trivial and yet significant examples: learning to walk and to talk. Ability to transport oneself and to communicate oneself linguistically provide greater opportunity and demand for relationship and unity. But they have been in turn achieved through relationship and unity, at first with those who guided one's early halting steps and taught one equally halting words, and subsequently in the continuous exchange within the many communities to which one belongs and which one encounters. New or deeper relationships in community are the ordinary means of growth in differentiation and freedom for the individual member.

The priority of the future

Let me return to the historical dimension. I suggested that the ethical consisted in the making of history which I still wished to describe in terms of higher human unity through deeper human differentiation – the making of community and the development of persons. Communities are made and persons developed in history.

The relation of history to moral decisions and behaviour, personal and communal, is frequently presented as the burden of the past or more neutrally as the setting of certain inherited preconditions within which moral options are available. In this undoubtedly authentic aspect of the relationship history as past is rather like the natural and biological as given. Freedom of decision and action is not precluded but the conditions of its exercise are set. History is seen as burden perhaps to the point of enslavement – as some people would see the history of Northern Ireland, for example. Or else history is ignored as bunk, as irrelevant as the Model T to today's Detroit automobile designer. In this case also the effect is destructive of real freedom as ignoring the laws of gravity is of air transport.

The context established by history in mental and social forces and structures, from language to the international economic order, is the context in which we must achieve and exercise our freedom and behave morally. Yet experience, history itself, teaches us that while these forces and structures may not be ignored, they may be harnessed to our advantage and our freedom. They may even be radically overcome. The decisively new can occur in personal and social history, maintaining no doubt a continuity with the past but establishing an observable discontinuity.

Subjects and objects of history

Further reflection on the moral goal of making history by freely developing person and community reveals that the moral subject, personal and communal, is called to become the subject of history not its object. By that I mean that the person or community is called to be determinative of history rather than determined by it. Elsewhere I have tried to show how this call applies in Northern Ireland.[7] The lessons from its history would look quite different if they were approached from the point of view of the people who tried to shape that history as its subjects rather than from the point of view of the people who now regard themselves, consciously or unconsciously, as inexorably shaped and determined by it as its objects. The subjectivisation of history as opposed to its objectivisation is the summons of ethics and above all of social ethics.

It would not be difficult to illustrate this in terms of the needs of the many marginalised people of our society and still more of the marginalised tribes and nations of the Third World. The ethics of economics and industry, of medicine and drugs or of communications, could all be illumined and enriched by considering the subjectivising thrust of a particular structure or practice as against any objectivising tendency. For the di-polarity of person and community in their moral endeavours, subject versus object analysis provides both clarification and a criterion of balance.

The problem of balance

The introduction of the concept of balance as between person and community might seem unnecessary in an analysis in which the development of the one sould seem to necessarily involve the development of the other. Such a conclusion would fail to take full account of the related concepts of provisionality and history as applied to ethical understanding and personal and social development. (A further and more influential reason will emerge shortly.) In any historical situation where ethical understanding and development are provisional, limited and unfinished, the two poles of person and community may be the subjects of unequal growth and development.

It is a matter of recorded experience that in different ages different stages of development applied to person and community and different balances were struck. In the fitful struggle in which mankind emerged with self-consciousness, deliberate freedom and history, this should cause no surprise. Yet at a particular time the balance struck may be too heavily weighted in favour of the individual person or the community. The revelation of such unfair weighting and its critique may be derived from considering how far person and community are subjects and objects of the historical process. If the members of the community are simply the objects of community decisions and not the subjects of their own history with proper participation in communal decisions, and adequate protection for development, the balance is wrong. If, on the other hand, there is a spirit of development where individuals seek complete freedom as subjects of their history, the community will either disintegrate and defeat their purpose or it will be taken over by the strong whose individual development will be sought at the expense of the weak. The past and the present are full of notorious examples of both kinds of imbalance.

Past, present and future

One conclusion of this discussion is that history, or at any rate the making of history, is about the future rather than about the past. It does not ignore the past because that establishes the resources and sets the conditions for future development, at least to a degree. We have noted the possibility of overcoming these conditions and transforming these resources in a radical break with the past. To deny this would be to reduce history to continuous evolution once again.

This attitude to history as properly future does not devalue the present. It is only through the present that we can come to the future or the future can come to us. To reach for or expect the future without any engagement with the present is to miss the future because it is to ignore the real demands of time as a process. It bears some resemblance to attempting to reach London from Manchester by stepping into the train compartment at

Piccadilly Station and walking right through on to the tracks beyond expecting it to be Euston. There is a waiting as there is a striving element in our temporal or historical condition. But there is no evading that condition as it moves from the past into the future through the present.

The present is the time for ethical action; the past sets certain conditions and provides certain resources but the future is its goal, the source of its challenge and call. A genuine ethics is future-oriented for person and community. The unity in differentiation may be partially achieved, or already exist; but that very given alerts, summons and impels us to what is yet to be achieved. Personal and social ethics – and they cannot be properly separated or even finally distinguished – are concerned with guidance and achievement for the future and not primarily with the preservation of the present or fidelity to the past. In that sense the future is the proper zone of freedom and morality for the person and community.[8]

Evil, tragedy, suffering, death

I cannot help feeling at once a certain security about the general validity of what I have been saying and a certain insecurity about a particular air of unreality, artificiality or abstraction. I recorded earlier my own dissatisfaction with an individualist ethics which abstracted the individual from his communal context. Compensating for that by stressing the equality of the social pole with the additional dimensions of nature and history does not quite remove my unease. And it is an unease which I have with much more powerful and influential moral analyses that this one.

It is an unease born of bracketing the evil, the tragedy, and the suffering and death in the world. Human reality is so complex that it is not possible to attend to everything at once, I grant. So matters have to be taken in some order, even at the risk of distorting them by isolating them for a time. (Time, history and provisionality are always with us.) I do not concede that moral or ethical analysis may finally ignore how far evil and tragedy, suffering and death, are structured into person and community and may dismiss them as unfortunate aberrations and addenda. The greatest limitation of personal ethical analysis in particular, as we find it for instance in the natural law tradition, is not its inadequate attention to the historical condition of man as moral agent – something understandable in classical writers like Aquinas – but its filtering out the evil and the tragic. At a certain ontological level of analysing being this may again be excusable, even acceptable (although I have my reservations). At the level of the practical science of morals it is not.

In the shadow of evil (which I will use in a general sense for the moment to include all the destructive aspects of reality) the di-polarity of person and community, the interaction of nature and freedom and the relations between past, present and future assume an ambiguity which qualifies all moral discernment, response and achievement.

Person and community may no longer be considered as simply mutually enriching or judged to be merely in need of some balancing corrective as temporarily out of phase in their development. The difficulty lies deeper, demands a more radical cure and may never be finally removed. The possibility of mutual enrichment which in that first and valid – because necessary – abstraction person and community offer one another, has its counterpoint in the mutual conflict and destruction of which they are also capable and to which certain forces constantly incline them. Unity and differentiation no longer spontaneously or even deliberately operate a creative dialectic. Unity is frequently achieved at the cost of differentiation by oppression of peoples and suppression of freedom. Differentiation threatens fragmentation of community where it is not exploited by the few at the expense of the many. Differences of race and nationality, of religion, of historical and educational background, of economic interest, of sex and family, frequently issue in destruction and exploitation rather than in greater differentiation, freedom and creativity in the fuller community. And the threat is always there.

It remains true that the direction of social ethics is towards deeper differentiation in unity, freedom in communion,[9] but it is a direction now under threat, and the formula has to be translated into a summons to promote differentiation in unity over threatened suppression of differentiation and the destruction of unity. The thrust towards the future remains but the inheritance of the past may, in its ambiguity as gift and threat, prove genuinely destructive as one endeavours to resolve the ambiguity in the present for the sake of a richer future. That richer future is not automatically or even consistently achieved. Regression is as much part of mankind's recorded history as progression. Social ethics has no illusions about a rosy future. High civilisations and their communities have disintegrated and died like their lowliest member.

Yet the summons to the future remains central to the understanding of social ethics. It will be a more uncertain and ambiguous future. The social moralist has no indication that that ambiguity and uncertainty will ever finally be resolved. Provisionality in achievement as in understanding seems the permanent lot of the analyst and agent in social ethics.

Social ethics and Christian faith

It seemed necessary to pursue this far the basis and structure of social ethics before discussing its relationship to and interaction with Christian faith. The outline has necessarily been rather general, but such an outline can be filled in later. And at its own level it seems to me to have a certain roundedness or completeness. But how does it connect with Christian faith, if it does?

In a previous discussion based on a rather restricted personal model I adopted the strategy of pursuing the underlying puzzles or difficulties which such an analysis of morality revealed.[10] Much of that strategy is still applicable. For example the ethical di-polarity of person-in-community and community-of-persons which gave rise to the criterion of higher unity through deeper differentiation depends on a certain irreducible character of both person and community. The irreducible and inviolable character of the person whereby he may not be simply used, suborned or eliminated by another or by the community[11] presents its own puzzle which is not amenable to further analysis by the moralist but calls for the metaphysician or theologian, or both, because it is a question of ultimate world view, religious or non-religious. The Christian acceptance of the God of Jesus Christ as the final absolute or of the absolute as God of Jesus Christ, with its correlevant understanding of man as created in the image of the absolute God and destined in Jesus Christ to share intimately as son and heir in that absolute mystery, provides at least a possible and coherent answer to the puzzle. More significantly for our purposes the Christian doctrines of creation and incarnation deal not just with the individual man but with mankind. Their vehicles have always been communities, from the stories of the origins of mankind in the first man and woman to the foundation of the people of Israel in Abraham to its election in the Exodus event to the emergence of the new people, the new mankind in Jesus Christ. The ultimately irreducible community is in this perspective – mankind created and redeemed by the Father in Jesus Christ. So any exclusiveness or discrimination, exploitation or neglect, in terms of race or sex, economics or geography, is a violation of this ultimate community and an impoverishment of all its members.

The freedom essential to the emergence of the human individual from animal to person and of the human group from herd to community presents its own puzzling features. For the moralist it is a datum. He finds it there. For the moralist curious beyond his own immediate terms of reference it is a question of his philosophy of life or religious belief. The creation doctrine relates human freedom to the human's particular place in creation. This freedom is reaffirmed, restored and transformed in the

new community established by the Incarnation,
Redemption and Resurrection of Jesus Christ into the
freedom of the children of God. The freedom, like the
sonship and the community, is both gift and task, given
and to be achieved. It has been inaugurated in what Jesus
described as the inbreaking of the Kingdom, an
anticipation of the future. The way of sons in free
community is into the future where the fullness of freedom
and sonship and community will be conferred on them.
For now the gift that is in them seeks its fullness in the
future through deeper differentiation and freedom and
fuller community, enjoying more fully the basic human
and Christian bond of community, love.

The fragility remains to be accounted for. In human
experience and moral struggle evil and rejection persist,
tragedy may prevail and at least death is a constant. By
what canon can one still feel summoned into future which,
if it does not include communal destruction, will certainly
include personal death with its threat of absurdity or at
least meaninglessness for everybody's moral striving?
That absurdity and meaninglessness were taken on by
Jesus Christ in his mortal life. Their apparent triumph
over him was their own final undoing. By his resurrection
Jesus broke the bonds of death and meaninglessness, not
least for our social moral enterprise.

The personal and communal gift and promise with
their summons to the final future provide the hope of
mankind's final subjectivisation. Man's call to become
subject of his history and not object is no longer doomed
to frustration. Although its realisation in history will
always be partial and erratic, the final fulfilments of
history or its transcendence in resurrection will allow

each one to be fully subject, fully differentiated and fully free in the eschatalogical community of the children of God.

Objections

In this hasty review of the relationships between social ethics and Christian faith, the pieces may have fitted together too easily and too neatly. Is this not the result of my Christian presuppositions determining the structure of my ethical analysis and so allowing me to solve a problem which never really existed? This objection needs, in true scholastic fashion, to be distinguished into two if not three parts.

Firstly, it must be conceded that one cannot simply divorce oneself from one's religious and particularly intellectual religious background in discussing issues of this kind. However, awareness of this could make one more sensitive to the danger of mishandling the evidence and distorting the analysis. The non-Christian analyst cannot shed his background and presuppositions either. He can only, like myself, try honestly and painstakingly to allow for them.

More important is the examination of the analysis in its own terms as an examination of the basis and structure of social ethics as it is encountered today without any explicit invoking of Christian data. That they may be implicitly influential would not be particularly significant. They are implicitly influential in the whole of western tradition of moral experience and analysis for two thousand years. How far do they enter into the UN Declaration of Human Rights for example? The basic question remains: is this analysis valid? If not, why not? As the examination papers say – you must give reasons for your answer. In this kind of dialogue it is possible to reach some clarification of position in a rational way which may allow for some rational choice between alternatives. I am not arrogant enough to think that this is the only valid moral analysis possible. I am too conscious of my own limitations and the provisionality of the whole exercise for that. There may be better or certainly preferable analyses available. But they will be better or preferable for reasons other than my or their author's Christian or non-Christian background.

I have laboured this part of my response to the objection because it is so commonly raised and seems finally irrelevant, an example of what somebody called the genetic fallacy, rife beyond the confines of this discourse. Its central stance seems to be that if you can trace or even suggest the hidden origins of somebody's position, you thereby undermine it.

However, I have a more serious reservation myself about the neatness and ease of the relationship between social ethics and Christian faith as depicted above. The singularity and depth of the particular puzzles were not sufficiently probed to convey the genuine sense of limitation and frustration which the moral analyst feels about these problems. Neither were the limitations and fragmentariness of our Christian understanding of God, absolute, creation, redemption, sonship, freedom, kingdom at all adequately conveyed. If they had been, the coherence or unity would not have been so neat, and the differentiation much deeper with consequent opportunity for greater mutual enrichment (and destruction). Some of these difficulties may be illuminated from other angles later in the book.

Notes

1   Compare Grenholm, C. H., *Christian Social Ethics in a Revolutionary Age* (Verbum, Uppsala, 1973).
2   See above: chapter 1, pp. 1–20.
3   Compare *Gift and Call* (Dublin–New York, 1975).
4   See above: chapter 1, p. 30.
5   The similarity to the ideas of Teilhard de Chardin on unity and differentiation as expounded in *The Phenomenon of Man* (London–New York, 1959), (cf. pp. 254ff.) is undoubted but not deliberately intended.
6   In later discussion I tend to refer 'community' to the more organically and biologically related human group or pattern of human relationships, and 'society' to the more deliberately chosen and fostered type of group or pattern of relationships. All human communities have some deliberative element. All human societies have an organic and biological substrate. The distinction is to some extent a matter of artificial definition and not relevant here.
7   Compare McDonagh, E., 'An Irish theology of liberation?' in Lane, D. (ed.). *Liberation Theology: An Irish Dialogue* (Dublin–New York, 1977).
8   Taking the future as the proper zone of morality forces no conclusion to the choice between a teleological, deontological or mixed model of ethics. Compare Frankena, W. F., *Ethics* (New Jersey, 1973).
9   The relationship between differentiation, freedom and community I have already discussed. Here I use the term 'communion' as stressing the achieved but yet dynamic unity of community within which the freedom of the members can be protected, exercised and developed.
10 Compare *Gift and Call*, chapter 4, 'Morality and Jesus Christ'; chapter 10 'Discerning God's action in the world'.
11 Compare *ibid.*, chapters 2 and 3.

Chapter Three

SOCIAL JUSTICE AND HUMAN RIGHTS

While the di-polarity of person-in-community and community-of-persons remains central to our search for a social ethics for Christians, it is time to define some more precise meaning or meanings of these terms. This applies in particular to the term 'community' which I have been employing in a very general sense from family to international community of states. Taking it as a generic description of any group of people united in a discernible and more or less defined pattern of relationships and so enabled to function together for specific purposes, I am well aware that each person belongs to a whole series of partly overlapping communities. So, John Smith is a member of a particular family, church, state, while at the same time he belongs to the factory community where he works, to his local trade union, to the Labour Party, to the local darts club and to a whole series of less defined patterns of relationship which constitute the local community. It is possible and necessary to select some of the more critical of these communities for fuller investigation, whilst bearing in mind that they do not exhuast the life, relationships and communities of John Smith. This is an important proviso because one of the temptations of all analysts, not least moral ones, is to confuse aspects of interest accessible to them with the whole of reality. In this study, three criteria of community are appropriate.

The first is a group's overarching importance and influence through its effect on other patterns of relationship or communities. This will obviously exclude the local darts club and similar recreational groups. However, voluntary communities of a social or political kind, which do not have the range or influence of state institutions, will be considered *in globo* in so far as they are distinct from and not reducible to state institutions.

The approach is secondly qualified by confining attention to such significant communities and patterns of relationship and function which are amenable to this kind of analysis. For that reason, I will ignore the worldwide English-speaking community, for example, and various other cultural groups of which the nation is in some sense the most significant.

The third criterion is more practical than theoretical. Due to limitations of time and space I will have to exclude some socially very significant communities like the family, the school or the work community (whether industrial, service or professional) from any extended analysis. I hope, however, that the discussion will fill out adequately the sketch of community and its ethical dimensions adopted in chapter 2, and by suitable illustration and modification be seen to be fruitful for a consideration of all important communities.

The political community of the state

In very many ways the political order with its pattern of relationships whereby people are united in a single *polis* or state as *politai* or citizens, and so function internally in pursuit of certain common purposes and, at the same time, interact externally with other states, establishes the most obvious of communities. To many members, observers and analysts past and present, it is also in its different expressions the most critical community.

The reasons for this are manifold. By guaranteeing, through its exclusive possession of the sanction of force, essential internal order and basic protection from external disturbance, the state, in whatever form, attends to the minimal requirements for human survival for its citizens. Nowadays, it must in fact be seen as involving a good deal more than some of its primitive ancestors or even than its sophisticated predecessors of the liberal kind in the nineteenth century conceived or achieved as its proper goal and function. At the same time it has also to be recognised as being a good deal less than certain earlier theorists and practitioners visualised it in terms of self-possession and self-sufficiency. The more relates basically to the increased role of the state in the internal economic and general welfare order. The less concerns its external relations and the growing interdependence between states. Paradoxically, its increased internal role and power, at least in the economic order, is paralleled by increased external dependence in the international economic order. The economic self-sufficiency and self-determination of states have been seriously and consciously diminished in recent times. The most powerful economic country of today, the USA, cannot escape this dependence, while some of the most crucial moral questions of our time concern the life-and-death dependence of some countries on the vagaries of international trade.[1]

The identifiable political community of the state, then, is constituted by a (changing) pattern of internal and external relations. In the past at least, and for some people still in principle, political relationships should be distinguished from economic, cultural and religious relationships, for example. The denial or affirmation and the understanding of these distinctions are crucial to basic political philosophy and the nature of a state. The marxist, the socialist, the liberal, the conservative and the fascist, to name but a few, will clearly divide on these issues. And it may well be asked if the enterprise of social ethics is not entirely ruled out until this prior question of political philosophy is settled.

That is undoubtedly a serious difficulty for the ethical analyst, perhaps more serious than the one earlier considered about his Christian or non-Christian presuppositions. The difficulty is compounded not only by the careless use of labels (like marxist, liberal, fascist) but by the very variety of political philosophies which might be grouped under any one of these labels. How far can we identify, for example, Soviet, Chinese and European communism with one another and with any of the particular textbook marxisms of which there is also a plurality?

Difficult as the objection is, and attractive as the prior study of and decision upon a particular political philosophy appears, the moral analyst has to make his own moral decision about proceeding with the enterprise of social ethics or not. He is at least encouraged to go on by the recognition that any systematic analysis, however profound and comprehensive, cannot hope to be more than provisional, open to further and continuing revision.

Secondly, many of the urgent problems in social ethics will not wait upon a total grasp of political philosophy, although they will be better served by a serious attempt to provide some systematic theoretical structure. Such a structure and even a full-scale political philosophy could not aspire to escape from our time-conditioned and provisional understanding into some land of the eternal verities.

Aware, then, of conscious and unconscious political presuppositions, and acknowledging the political as well as intellectual and ethical traditions within which one works, I console myself that they will be more fully revealed in the actual ethical analysis itself and so may be more easily criticised and taken account of. So, I feel emboldened to proceed with my analysis of social ethics and its critical confrontation with Christian faith.[2]

The acceptance of the state as one sharpening of the focal point, community, with its correlative focus of person as citizen, enables one to examine more precisely principles like unity through differentiation and freedom in communion introduced in the previous chapter. This must, however, take into account the natural–biological, the historical and creative and tragic backgrounds of the poles of person–citizen and community–state, and also place them in the wider interstate context.

Citizen and state: differentiation and unity

Differentiation and unity as applied to the roles of the citizen and state provide certain general guidance which may be expressed by certain value-terms. For example, the state's attention to the differentiation embodied in the individual citizens must respect their unique and irreducible character as persons, otherwise their human dignity. State activity in its legislative, administrative and judicial functions, as performed of course by its functionaries, may not ignore or disrespect this human value and dignity. The more precise implications of this dignity and the appropriate responses to it in differing contexts require a lot of detailed work, but some immediate consequences could be expected by consistent attention to this dignity in regard to more vulnerable citizens such as the ill, the handicapped, the aged, children, the racially different, the homosexual, the unemployed and the poor, and in relation to other marginalised people such as prostitutes, alcoholics, drug addicts, or petty criminals and prisoners of all kinds. Sensitivity to these vulnerable people's undeniable and inalienable human dignity will provide a fairly severe test of the ethical awareness expressed in state structures and manifested by their agents.

This awareness of and concern for the ultimate worth of the individual citizen does not admit of distinction or discrimination. Equal concern and respect for every individual citizen must also characterise the structure and operations of the state.[3] This may be institutionalised in various ways and may to some extent be expressed as equality before the law. It will exclude in our present understanding, practices that are discriminatory on the basis of sex, religion or race. Once again, the more detailed provisions cannot be gone into here and the historical perception and expression of this equality may not be reduced to some abstract eternal truth. The

equality in question has been discerned and institutionalised slowly and painfully in human history and
the process is far from complete.

This respect and concern for the citizens with its
associated equality is not to be understood in the kind of
mutual or negative way suggested in the discussion about
'negative liberty' by Isaiah Berlin[4] and others. Apart from
the practical and theoretical difficulties which I believe
Berlin's position to involve in regard to the notion of
liberty itself, it is clear that the state today has, or (as I
hope to show) ought to have, a much more positive
attitude towards its citizens. By this I mean that the state
does and should ensure for all its citizens the resources
and opportunities as well as the necessary protection from
interference by others, essential to their personal
historical development, their growth in differentiation
and creativity. Without such positive provision, its
concern for their character as persons would be merely
verbal and clearly unequal in its results, as the strong
would flourish at the expense of the weak.

The present positive attitude and activity of the state, at
least in western countries, has derived perhaps less from
doctrinaire philosophies of statehood than it has been
haltingly and painfully developed in response to needs of
the weak and exploited who could no longer be ignored.
The progress still to be made in regard to the vulnerable
and marginal groups I touched on briefly above.

Positive role of the state and social welfare

In an effort to structure this response of the state to the
citizen it may be useful to consider him or her again as a

biological organism which may become over time and in a social context the differentiated, creative and free being we call a person, remaining all the while open to and in need of further development and yet subject to hurt, failure, frustration and ultimately to organic and historical disintegration in death.

As an organic or natural and biological being, which the person for all his subsequent developments and achievements never ceases to be, the person/citizen requires nutrition, warmth, shelter, rest. At critical times in this life he is clearly unable to provide these for himself – when he is very young, old or ill. In our complex society individual families and neighbours are frequently in no position to take on the burdens of supplying these physical needs. So some degree of organised help is called for, and this becomes more pressing and extensive in the great urban concentrations of our time. If the citizenry as a whole and the institutions of state with their consent and at least financial support did not operate a system for the care of the young, the ill (including the physically and mentally handicapped) and the old, then the basic respect for human dignity in its need for survival would be lacking from the state in relation to a great many people and so lacking in its entirety. This kind of respect is in principle indivisible even if scarcity of resources or mismanagement of them or ignorance may be sometimes alleged in excuse of failure. The principle is clear. The community, organised as a state and called to respect the differentiation and dignity of all, has to respond in an organised way to the basic physical needs at least of those members unable to provide for themselves.

A few further clarifications are in order. Such inability

of the individual to provide may not be due to physical and mental disability through age or illness or handicap – straightforward individual disability as it were. There may also be a social disability based on lack of education or employment or any of the social privations and discriminations from race to geography which affect the structures of our society. These are no less the concern of the community and its state-structures.

State provision, on the other hand, may not be fine enough and sensitive enough to cope with everybody in need within the run of its writ. So, there may be need of voluntary activity by individuals and groups to supplement the statutory services. Whether the role of voluntary services in this and other areas is upheld as a matter of principle or simply emergency practice, depends on the overall character of the state and its basic political philosophy.

The ethical point to note is the community's responsibility to provide for the primary physical needs of its members and in our world the necessary, if not the exclusive role of the state in this.

The state and international welfare

The physical needs of its own members do not today exhaust the ethical responsibilities of the community in this field. The inter-linking of states in what is sometimes called the 'international community' demands the moral awareness of and the moral responsibility to the much greater physical needs which exist beyond the particular western state or the whole affluent world. Two out of three people in the world at large lack the necessary food and water, some two billion people suffer from malnutrition, with ten million children in direct danger of death.[5] The existing links of communication and distribution, the resources actually available and the dreadful gulf in standard of living and dying, present a clear and present obligation for the affluent communities and states to respond urgently and effectively. Short-term emergency help and long-term removal of the causes of this imbalance, such as lack of necessary technical skill and technology, are both required.

A more serious demand is the radical reform of international structures, particularly economic and trading structures, which at present are clearly designed to make the strong stronger and the weak weaker. To ignore this clear and present obligation or to make the merely token response which most western states permit themselves, is to deny in action what is affirmed in word about the recognition and respect due to one's own citizens as human beings. The hungry billions are no less human, no less worthy of recognition and respect, no less covered by the indivisible principle of respect for all. There exist structured relationships with them and so responsibilities to them. All that is lacking is the effective will.

Negative respect for human life

Having given so much time and space to the positive response called for to the physical needs of citizens and others, I may be forgiven for a rather brief reference to the negative side of that primary and positive moral duty summarised as respect for human life. The protection of that life from the assaults of others is obviously part of the community responsibility nominally exercised by the state's officers of public order.

Such a need and the still wider need of protecting the citizens and their institutions of state from destruction in war expose the shadow and tragic side of human existence. In the broken world in which we live, security forces, prisons and armies are necessary. Yet the very call to protect men in their physical existence may not be used as an excuse for simply eliminating or degrading other men. Wars of defence may still be necessary and justified. So may revolutions against intolerable tyranny. But these are last resort responses and a great deal more effort and resources must go into the study of alternative methods of settling international disputes, providing adequate national defence, overcoming tyrannous oppression and achieving social change in face of grave exploitation. In the fight against crime, torture or inhuman and degrading treatment in the police-cell or the prison are an assault on human beings and their dignity and rather an endorsement and prolongation of criminal activity than a protection against it. It is difficult to see how capital punishment can uphold the community's sense of value of life and the dignity of the human being or whence the community or state derives the authority to take life in such circumstances.

The long hard road to combining adequate protection for law-abiding citizens with proper concern for and treatment of those accused or convicted of crime is one of the more urgent if less dramatic tasks of ethics, politics and the law. The much more difficult and dramatic task of finding effective alternatives to violence as a means of political change or conservation within a state or between states amounts to one of the great moral demands of our time. In this context the care of the hungry is the other immediate and long-term goal.

Abortion and euthanasia

Remaining still with the protection of human life, one could and should discuss problems of abortion and euthanasia. However, they are such particular questions and receive so much detailed discussion,[6] if not exactly in the context of social ethics properly considered, I will content myself with posing some neglected questions.

How far do the critics and opponents of abortion and euthanasia combine with their advocates and practitioners in defining and clarifying areas of agreement about respect for human beings and human lives, on which both seem to me ultimately to rest their case? How far do they combine to seek practical, positive and creative alternatives to negative and even violent solutions? However sophisticated the techniques, there is a measure of forcible extinction of life in both abortion and euthanasia which might be fairly described as violent. Finding and implementing alternatives which might be both socially desirable and personally acceptable would of course make greater demands on the advocates, opponents and community at large.

These demands may vitally affect the future of society, and social ethics is concerned above all with the future. For the sake of that future we must ask: how far do a policy and practice of abortion and euthanasia affirm and respect the differentiation and so the dignity and eventual freedom of the human being, which must begin as a tiny but differentiated organic unit, develop into a more or less recognisable human being and lapse in turn with organic disintegration? And how far do they deny and degrade that differentiation? And even that slightly extended note omits any reference to the tragic dimension of human existence, and how it bears on the questions of both general policy and particular decisions.

Human development and state activity

The differentiation of the human being is not exclusively or even primarily 'natural' or 'biological'. Becoming a person – which is one way of describing the characteristic life task of the human being – involves the interaction of biological nature, emotion, intelligence and freedom, of individual and group, of past, present and future. The group over time, by sharing its insights and achievements with an individual, assists him in the integration of the physical, emotional and intellectual into the (partially) self-aware, self-possessed and self-disposing unit we call a person.

In this task too the state has increasingly understood its role as making available as effectively and fairly as possible the cultural, intellectual and other resources of the community, its insights and achievements, in assisting each of its citizens to reach the fullness of development. Its recognition of the equal dignity of and concern for all, demands of the state not merely a negative or even supplementary role but a positive and institutional role.

How far this may issue in any pattern of schools or school curriculum is a matter of debate for times, places and eventually political philosophies. What seems morally clear is that only the state can today provide the necessary resources, that such provision does not automatically entitle it to total control and uniformity in organisational pattern and still less to impose a single narrow indoctrinating curriculum. Such an approach collapses the educational dimension of mankind into the political. It fails to accept a distinction crucial to respect and concern for differentiation of its citizens as persons, and so the differentiation within them between citizenship with its rights and duties and wider dimensions of human living and thinking and acting that can never be simply reduced to the political.

The differentiation in unity relating person and community, and so citizen and state, is operative within the person as it distinguishes and unites citizen and person. That much seems to me central to this approach to social ethics.

Beyond citizenship and the state

It is his ability, need and freedom to act outside the political context so structurally defined and to enter into or establish networks of relationships that are not state-imposed or controlled, that reveal the person as transcending the citizen and the community as transcending the state. If one were to use for this total network of relationships and contexts coterminous in people and territory with a particular state, the word 'society', then the distinction of state and society and the view of the state as more restricted than society would be a means of expressing this ethical base.

Activities in and of this society are in an obvious sense subject to the laws of the state with its obligations to respect and show concern for the citizen. The laws of the state contradict their own true role when they fail to show that respect and concern in ignoring or suppressing the differentiated character of the individual citizen as person, of his various relationships, groups and activities or by discriminating in these in favour of some groups and against others. Equality of treatment for all under the law, and respect for basic freedom by the law, offer a contemporary shorthand for this responsibility of the state and its instrument the law.

Human rights[7]

It is at this juncture that the question of human rights should be discussed. (Again I may be excused for skimping such an important issue by adverting to the extensive and valuable discussion of all this now in progress among lawyers, politicians, philosophers and theologians. However, some comment is necessary to set the question in the context of my wider discussion.)

These basic rights derive eventually from the di-polarity of person and community, then translated into citizen and state and so expressed in legal protection and demand. This is not to reduce such rights to the merely legal to be granted at the discretion of the state-power, which would remove their character as human rights altogether.

The di-polarity and the recognition, respect and concern of the state for the differentiation and dignity of citizen based on his personal worth, require various institutionalisations. However, such respect and institutionalisations have a history and the history is like all history, incomplete and will never be completed. Here the recent western democratic tradition has proved decisive as far as civil and political liberties or human rights are concerned.

The most famous example of this is the United Nations Declaration in 1948. The recognition of such rights, their more precise formulations and final institutionalisation in international agreements and domestic law, develop through history. We may be grateful to the history which has recognised such critical freedoms as that of assembly, association and speech. Their widespread recognition is no guarantee that they are respected. Similar rights, to fair trial for example or against arbitrary arrest and various kinds of discrimination, although widely acknowledged in theory, are very vulnerable in practice. The convenient device of the emergency has led to serious flouting of civil rights even in countries that pride themselves on their tradition of fair play and respect for the person and the law. Social and economic rights are much less developed as practical instruments in Western thought and practice and may prove the stumbling block or launching pad to radical social change.

The historical character of human rights in their recognition and institutionalisation does not mean that they are simply reversible and have no real and permanent moral base. It simply recognises the character of their origins, their continuing historicity in being open to being flouted or conveniently forgotten, but more important in being open to further refinement and development. Consistent with a social ethics oriented to the future, the understanding and implementation of human rights constitute an unfinished task and a summons to the richer future.

In some ways in their current formulations human rights resemble conciliar definitions or dogmas of the church, expressing a certain grasp of the truth, frequently formulated in time of crisis to exclude the misleading or erroneous, but historically conditioned themselves and open to revision, refinement and completion if not simple reversal of the sense in which they were originally intended. Such conciliar definitions are again signposts for the future rather than remnants of the past.

The struggle for human rights, for this fuller recognition and faithful implementation, is part of the social moral task of all communities and states, all persons and citizens. It is a decisive struggle in upholding the state's respect for the distinction between state and society.

The economic order

What to many people is the most obvious and even most important aspect of the relationships of state, society and the range of human rights has so far received no more than a passing mention – the economic order of society. So much government activity is today concerned with economics that one might be forgiven for concluding that politics is simply about economics, that the political order may be reduced to the economic at least in the sense that the economic takes precedence over and determines the range and significance of all other political activity.

The power of the economic in politics can scarcely be

overestimated. Yet to collapse politics into economics would be a very serious impoverishment with obvious implications for human rights. It is as likely to happen through attitudes and informal practices as through institutional changes. (The consumer society comes close enough to it.) The distinction might be upheld by saying that the economic order was entirely subordinated to and integrated into the political, but that the political dealt with much wider concerns than that. More narrowly still it might demand that the political controlled the economic at least by public ownership of the means of production. And we can move along these lines through the various blends of mixed economy so widespread today to an entirely free market economy (mainly a theoretical concept today). The exploitation of labour and injustice and distribution which the capitalist system and (partially) free market economy have caused, have become increasingly clear to us in this century. That we are far from the end of such degradation the Third, Fourth and Fifth Worlds forcibly remind us.

Such an economic order, given its inherent structure of injustice in terms of disrespect of man even in his physical needs, is no longer an acceptable moral option. Where along the rest of the spectrum one should make one's choice demands very careful analysis and evaluation. There may be a plurality of choices called for in different countries. There may be short term and long term choices. But reform of the economic order not just marginally but radically is becoming an increasingly urgent moral task, to which we must all contribute in different ways but above all through reform of internal and external political structures.[8]

Participation

The obligation to contribute to reforming the economic
order, particularly through political structures,
introduces my last point in this analysis of the di-polarity
of state and citizen. Hitherto the emphasis has been on the
state as recogniser and provider and co-ordinator,
although the relations were always clearly correlations
with reciprocal rights and duties.

The citizen's capacity and responsibility to contribute
to the operation of the state clearly does not stop at
obeying state law and paying state taxes. His condition as
person-in-community defined here in citizenship terms
underlines his capacity, his freedom and his obligation to
contribute. He will be denied his real human dignity if the
opportunity for this is denied him. He will be acting in a
manner inconsistent with his call to deeper differentiation
in higher community if he refuses to take an interest in
and to participate in the decisions about his own life,
which must to some extent be channelled through the
state. Varying degrees of participation are clearly possible
and actual at the present time. However, the main point of
this argument is the citizen's right and obligation to
participate in community decisions as exercised through
the state and the state's obligation to respect that right.

Social values and the just society

The ethical structures of relationships between citizen
and state, between citizen and citizen within the state,
and between states, which have been suggested here could
be expressed in what are called value terms, terms which

mediate the worthwhile or valuable moral character of the goals promoted by these structures or of the actions deriving from them.

The most obvious and traditional of these social values is justice. The ethically good society will be a just society and its state structures and activities will embody that social justice. Social justice demands, in line with the classical tradition of justice of giving every man his due, that the state should manifest and express its respect and concern equally for all its citizens. This respect and concern demands an ordered existence of peace under the law, attention to physical, educational and economic needs, participation in decision making and protection of certain basic rights and liberties. In its external relations it is no less bound to peace under the law, to attending on behalf of its citizens to the needs of the particularly deprived abroad, and to seeking such changes in the international order, including the economic order, as this may require.

Beyond the rather comprehensive value of social justice, at home and abroad, one can distinguish such values as peace, personal liberty, responsibility of participation and human solidarity. There is no agreed set of terms and no agreed enumeration. What is important to agree is the character and structure of the just society at home and abroad in its developing and historical condition with the correlative ideas of freedom in solidarity or communion.

How social values illuminate Christian faith

I do not think it would be particularly profitable to

rehearse once again the connections between the structure of social ethics, as applied here to the state–citizen di-polarity, and the structures of Christian faith. There would inevitably be an amount of tedious repetition. Instead I propose to reverse the process. Instead of asking Christian faith what it has to offer social ethics by way of confirmation or illumination or final significance, I shall begin at least by asking social ethics as outlined here what it has to offer in the development of faith, of the acceptance and understanding of the God of Jesus Christ in his saving activity.

Provisionality and unconditionality, gift and achievement

One must begin by acknowledging once again the provisionality of our present understanding and achievement and yet the unconditionality of our commitment to act out of the understanding we have and thereby correct and improve it in an unending dialectic of theory and praxis. This is our human condition as it emerges in social ethics at any rate.

One of the obvious questions to our Christian faith is: Does our faith reflect the same provisionality of understanding and unconditionality of commitment? Can these be kept in reasonable and permanent tension by the Christian? Can we expect to grow in understanding in the faith through praxis? If we can, what counts as praxis for the faith and how does such praxis illuminate our understanding? Is not all this suggesting that faith is a human achievement, perhaps a human projection and not a divine gift at all? If it is a divine gift and not a human achievement, is it not entirely at variance with basic human structures as they emerge in ethical analysis, and so to be written off as irrational and 'heroic', as some kind of leap or wager?

Perhaps the question ought now to be posed in the other direction by asking how far the understanding and achievement in social ethics is simply human achievement and not gift. And here we encounter a further mystery of human existence, knowledge and achievement, that it is given or received as much as it is achieved. The source of the gift may be beyond our ken, but, beginning with physical biological existence and its needs which have originally all to be supplied, and moving through the psychological and social development of the child, we see how far he is primarily a receiver. Of course, at his best, at his human best, he becomes a responsive even creative receiver not just a passive receptacle for various commodities from milk to love to knowledge.

This creative capacity enables him in turn to contribute creatively to others and to the community so that the gifts of the community available to present and future generations are maintained and extended. Creative receptivity leading to creative response and contribution to the community do not provide a bad model for the faith which we receive in the Christian community of believers, which grows in understanding and commitment within that community and contributes in turn to the community's fuller understanding and commitment. And the growth in understanding comes about not merely by formal learning, but also through the critical activity of Christian prayer and the exercise of the characteristic Christian responses of trust and love for God and

neighbour, indeed for God through neighbour. That is
the understanding of praxis which itself is generated by
the dynamic recognition and understanding of the
presence or gift of the God of Jesus Christ.

To some extent the mutual illumination suggested by
that comparison of faith and social ethics might be in
danger of sliding one into the other. And that would
certainly be false to the faith and indeed to the approach
to social ethics I have been attempting in this book. Can
one evade such reductionism and yet avoid the total
dichotomy of a reasonable ethics and an irrational faith?

Let us return to the centrepiece of this chapter's
analysis – the di-polarity of person and community as
expressed in the more confined relationship of citizen and
state. One of the more important points I argued for was
at once the essential, and central character of this
relationship, and the error of making it exhaustive of the
whole person–community di-polarity.

There are dimensions of the human, personal and
communal, which cannot be regulated by the law or
diminished by the bureaucrats. One of these is clearly any
ultimate overall philosophical or religious view of reality.
We as Christians and particularly Catholics may have
been obtuse and reluctant in discerning this and its
implications clearly, with our constantinian, mediaeval,
reformation and counter-reformation hang-ups. And
there are people and states including supporters and
opponents of religion, who do not concede it now.
Precisely in its transcending the objectives, the functions
and the network of the state as I have presented them here
in the context of social ethical analysis, religious faith
cannot be reduced to the ethical demands of good

citizenship or, as we saw in a previous chapter, to social ethical demands *tout court.*

Indeed, the recognition of these distinctions is essential not just to the preservation of the truly ethical character of ethics, which might otherwise become merely a means to some religious purpose, but also to the preservation of the liberties of the individual by insisting at once and radically that as a man's religious faith or non-faith transcends the state's limits, his religious freedom is not granted by and may not be revoked by state law. This, of course, is a further confirmation of the distinction between state as a limited pattern of relationships and structures for specific purposes, and society or community as the total set of relationships and institutions within the same geographical boundaries. The relation of religious faith and society is a matter for another chapter. I merely repeat the conclusions of the previous chapter that faith is not reducible to ethics or culture.

A final word on the human rights of which a conspicuous example is religious liberty. Apart from the not entirely fanciful parallel in origin and function between such rights and Christian doctrines, there is a sense in which the gradual discovery, protection and exercise of such rights enriches our faith, our awareness of, acceptance of and understanding of God. Such rights in so far as they accurately reflect in the historical process dimensions of man's true being, his capacities and his needs, and above all his future, provide in the light of our Christian doctrines of creation, redemption and resurrection the *vestigia Dei* which are as much anticipations of the Lord that is to come (*vestigia Dei advenientis*) as traces of the Creator God (*vestigia Dei creantis*).

Human rights or freedoms then provide a *locus theologicus*, which is necessarily obscure and changing. Yet given the limitations of our other *loci* for understanding or talking about God and his activity they may not be readily ignored.[9]

The development of a social ethics for Christians should increase not only their understanding of morality and of man but also their understanding of the God to whom they are coming in establishing the just society, or more correctly the God who is coming to them. But that is another story for another chapter.

Notes

1 The concept of dependence, particularly economic, is critical to the basically marxian analysis of their situation which has led Third World theologians to the concept of 'liberation' as key to their theological understanding. (See below, chapter 4, note 8 for fuller reference.) It has not, however, led to their attempt at a systematic social ethics for Christians of the kind projected here. Compare McDonagh E., 'The challenge of liberation theology' in *Liberation Theology: An Irish Dialogue* (Dublin–New York, 1977), pp. 22–34.

   At the political level the various UNCTAD conferences have been attempting vainly to deal with the problems of trade between First and Third Worlds, where the relationship domination–dependence clearly ought to yield to some kind of equal interdependence.

2 The basic values of social justice and personal freedom to which the title of this chapter refers, and which are unpacked in detail later on, undoubtedly reflect the main streams of political philosophy affecting at least western political thinking today. Social justice in analysis and aspiration is greatly influenced by the work of Marx and his predecessors. The analysis of freedom is ultimately rooted in certain Greek and Christian ideas but heavily influenced by the events, programmes, prophets and interpreters of the American and French Revolutions. A direct confrontation and extended dialogue

with these traditions is undoubtedly necessary for the fuller understanding of the basis and programme of a social ethic for Christians. Here one has to be content, not least for reasons of time and space, with the indirect confrontation and implicit dialogue.

3 Much of the subsequent analysis has clearly been influenced by discussion provoked by the work of John Rawls, which itself is in the individualist and libertarian tradition and takes less account of the socialist than I regard necessary. Compare Rawls, J., *A Theory of Justice* (Cambridge, Mass., 1971); Barry, B., *The Liberal Theory of Justice* (Oxford, 1973); Daniels, N. (ed.), *Reading Rawls* (Oxford, 1975); Wolff, R., *Understanding Rawls* (Princeton, 1977); Wren, B., *Education for Justice* (London, 1977). For a more traditional, scholastic type discussion compare Pieper, J., *The Four Cardinal Virtues* (Notre Dame, Ind., 1966).

4 Berlin, I., 'Two concepts of liberty' in *Four Essays in Liberty* (Oxford, 1969). One of the most painstaking and effective criticisms of this position which I have come across was produced by Charles Taylor in his lectures at All Souls, Oxford in the Michaelmas Term 1977.

5 Compare Power, J., and Holstein, A. M., *World of Hunger* (London, 1976).

6 Compare McDonagh, E., 'The ethics of abortion' in *Invitation and Response* (Dublin–New York, 1972).

7 Amongst recent accounts and analyses of human rights I found the following helpful: Brownlie, I., (ed.), *Basic Documents on Human Rights* (Oxford, 1971), Dworkin, R., *Taking Rights Seriously* (London, 1977); Falconer, A., 'The Christian and human rights' in *Doctrine and Life*, February 1978; Falconer, A., 'The churches and human rights' in *One in Christ*, No. 4, 1977; Moltmann, J., *The Church in the Power of the Spirit* (London, 1977); International Commission of Jurists, *Human Rights in a One-Party State* (London, 1978).

8 The significance of the economic order and its influence on political structures and decisions is undoubtedly critical to social ethics and raises once again the question of political philosophy, making the dialogue with Marxism, for example, more necessary than ever. Yet, it is, I believe, necessary to preserve the distinctions of the political and economic and social, and of citizen, economic man and person if the true relationships of differentiation and unity in economics as in other spheres is to be increasingly achieved. That is the main purpose of the present generalised discussion. One of the more helpful recent treatments with reference to Christian responsibility is: Wogaman, J. P., *Christians and the Great Economic*

Debate (London, 1977). Compare Sleeman, J. F., *Economic Crisis, A Christian Perspective* (London, 1976); Lindquist, M., *Economic Growth and the Quality of Life* (Helsinki, 1975). The argument has taken a new turn with the projection of a New International Economic Order. For some Christian response to this see the special issue of *Church Alert*, September–October 1977.

9 An obvious example of this is the growing recognition of the dignity, equality and rights of women which is clearly incompatible with some of the patriarchal ideas of God which have been so influential in the past.

Chapter Four

HUMAN SOCIETY AND THE KINGDOM OF GOD

The previous chapter discussed the God to whom men are coming in building a just society, or, more accurately, the God who is coming to them. In this chapter I wish to pursue this theme more fully under the rubric 'Human society and the kingdom of God'.

The historical background to this theme is too long and tangled in the Judaeo-Christian tradition for adequate discussion here. The biblical roots in Israel, in the preaching of Jesus and of the early Christian community[1] have sprouted a veritable jungle of interpretations and applications from Augustine's *De Civitate Dei*, the mediaeval synthesis of Christendom, and Luther's Two Kingdoms to recent views such as the Christian socialism of F. D. Maurice and his associates, the American Social Gospel, the more contemporary Christian–marxist dialogue and the largely South American phonemenon of Liberation Theology. And these are only some of the more significant references to a rich, if confusing, history.

Confusion has been mainly caused by varying understandings of the two poles 'human society' and 'kingdom of God'. This variation in understanding is part of the historicity of mankind, reinforced by the thorough-going historical character of the first of these poles,

human society. It would be naive to expect that the
confusion can be completely sorted out in our time or that
the understanding achieved or relationship sought could
escape the provisionality of our human, historical
achievements. None the less it is important to attempt
again the best understanding and most fruitful
relationship possible in the here and now. We may leave it
to others to reject or revise as they think necessary in the
there and then.

The Catholic and Protestant approaches

A footnote to recent historical developments may be of
particular interest in this ecumenical setting. The fresh
impetus to Christians tackling the social question in the
nineteenth and into the twentieth century issued in two
basically but not totally diverse approaches. One
approach which may be loosely described as Protestant
took the faith and theology, and particularly its
understanding of the Kingdom, as starting point. This
applied very strongly to the American Social Gospel
movement and with some qualifications to its English
predecessors in 'Christian Socialism'.[2] It has
characterised a great deal of outstanding Protestant
thinking and acting since, from Barth to Moltmann.[3] The
other approach, which may be loosely called Catholic,
started more from the pole of human society and the
ethics of that society understood in natural law terms.
This was particularly true of the Roman Catholic strand
which received its first official expression in the
encyclicals of Leo XIII and was continued by his
successors Pius XI, John XXIII and Paul VI in

particular.[4] And it characterised the work of such towering Anglican figures as William Temple.[5]

Despite the inevitable crude simplification, the distinction, I believe, is largely true or has been largely true up to very recently. The invaluable work of the World Council of Churches in this field in the last decades, including not only Anglican advisers like Ronald Preston and David Jenkins but heirs to a more strictly Protestant tradition in John C. Bennett and Heinz-Dietrich Wendland, has developed a concept of 'the responsible society' which is very much in the natural law tradition.[6]

On the other hand the emergence of Liberation Theology in South America[7] and to a lesser extent of political theology[8] in Europe has been a largely Catholic phenomenon and taken a theological rather than a natural law starting point. It has been directly concerned with God's activity and reign in the world, the coming of his kingdom.

The first point of this digression is to emphasise once again the artificiality of many of our theological and ecclesiastical divisions as far as Christian understanding, witness and service are concerned. The second is to reveal the search for a social ethics and for a correct understanding of society and kingdom as an ecumenical or inter-church task. It was partly for such reasons that I chose this topic for my Ferguson lectures.

The human phenomenon of society

With many reservations and without any wish to endorse uncritically either the Catholic natural law or Protestant kingdom approach, I prefer to abide by my original method here and consider first of all the human phenomenon of society. From diverse points of view this has been my continuous preoccupation throughout this book.

In the last chapter in particular, while I concentrated on that particular expression of society called the state, I insisted on the ultimate distinction between state and society and refused to accept any reduction of one to the other. Without some such distinction I do not see how one can define and defend fundamental human rights or liberties. Without it it is very difficult to uphold the irreducible di-polarity of person and community on which the whole axis of social ethics (as I understand it) rests. Deeper differentiation in fuller unity or freedom in communion cannot be properly pursued or achieved in a society totally identified with the political order and organisation of the state.

To uphold the distinction of state and society does not, however clear an idea of the state one has, enable one completely to define what one means by society. In an earlier discussion I used the word 'community' in a global and flexible way to provide for the biological/emotional as well as the 'deliberately' social and historical bonds whereby people are interconnected and to allow for the range of connections and groupings, received and achieved, from family to state to international community, from cultural and linguistic grouping to religious to recreational. Society may be used in equally global and flexible terms although I prefer to confine it to the social and historical groupings where the emphasis is on the element of human decision, however minimal.

Two concrete examples may help to illustrate the

intention and limitations of my concept of society. The biological–emotional bonds of parent and child may be and should be transformed through time into social relations by personal decision and commitment expressed in loving care. Parents become parents in the full human sense over time by 'deliberate' choice, but clearly the biological–emotional provides the normal basis and context and it is in turn expressed in the more human relations of a family that becomes in this sense a society.[9] Similarly a particular ethnic group in a particular territory transforms its biological–emotional ties into cultural patterns and social structure.[10]

My concern, then, as a moral analyst is with human relationships and groupings as they are an achievement of human deliberation, decision and freedom. But that can only occur and be understood, I must still insist, within the context of mankind as biological and emotional, bound by temporal, historical character, inexorably subject to the risk of pain, failure and tragedy as well as to the final and certain disintegration of death. Without continuous attention to these dimensions of human life and society the deliberation, decision and freedom and the social ethics invoked to guide them will become irrelevant abstractions.

This understanding of society provides some framework for considering such different and more or less defined societies as the family or the nation, the total pattern of relationships co-terminous with the organisation of a particular state as well as the wider pattern of entities such as western Europe or western society or the pattern of relationships of all mankind in a global society. It is to this varying complex of patterns that the dynamic of social justice developed in the last chapter, largely in relation to the state or inter-state grouping, more fully applies. From the microcosm of more particular patterns such as the family, the factory or the university to the macrocosm of a global society or societies, the call to build the just society of the future through respect, equality, freedom and participation resounds. What is the Christian significance of such call and response?

Theology of the kingdom

Certainly the Christian symbol most invoked for discerning the significance of a developing just society of mankind is that of God's kingdom or reign or rule. We have seen some of the confusing history of such invocation in the past. In the wake of so much recent biblical study of and insight into this aspect of the teaching of Jesus it behoves the theologian to tread warily. This applies in particular to the theologian of ethics because it is to the late-nineteenth-century reduction of the kingdom to some kind of human moral achievement that the biblical scholars reacted most violently. And on this much at least they now share and command agreement.[11]

The symbol of the kingdom or reign of God preached by Jesus and which came out of his Jewish background signified first and above all the achievement of God and not of mankind. It is primarily the coming of God, his coming in human history, his rule of men's hearts and minds, attitudes and action, persons and societies, and it is the decisive, final, eschatological coming of God to reign over mankind according to his promise. Moral achievement by the steady progress of mankind through history does not do justice to the divine initiative or to the disjunction as opposed to continuous progress which it introduces into human affairs and human history.

While for Jesus this kingdom is certainly future, it is also 'at hand', anticipated, 'beginning to realise itself', inaugurated in the event of Jesus himself, his person, his life, his actions and his words. The words of preaching and teaching in the summons to repentance and in the parables; the signs of exorcism, healings and forgiveness of sins, reveal this 'already' as well as the 'not yet' status of the kingdom. The completion of the 'already' stage was recognised by his early disciples in the events of the Death and Resurrection. His surrender to the powers of the law, sin and death which opposed God's kingdom provided the opportunity for God to triumph definitively over these powers in raising up Jesus to new life, a new life to be recognised and appropriated by the new mankind.

Although the final completion of God's coming in the Parousia was imminently expected by many in those early days, the basic inauguration accomplished by God in Jesus Christ established the double tension which the first Christian community experienced — between what has been accomplished in Jesus Christ with its implications for life and man's actual lifestyle, between what is already achieved by God and what is yet to come. The gift and grace, the presence of the Spirit of God sent by Jesus Christ whereby the kingdom is already realising itself, involves a call to mankind to live in accordance with that dignity which in human history has attained and still attains pitifully partial expression.

The presence of the Kingdom is judgment upon us as

well as gift to us. We are sustained only by the continuing promise, the future and final coming, the final reign of God in his untrammelled presence and power. It is not for us to know the day or the hour of this final coming. It has not entered into our hearts what the manner and content of that final coming shall be. (The apocalyptic descriptions in Mark 13 and parallels have to be treated with appropriate scholarly caution.) Yet some hints are available. The first fruits of that coming matured in the Resurrection of Jesus Christ whereby he broke through history to overcome death. He thereby achieved that fullness of presence to the Father which involves fullness of presence to his creation, including us, although we are still incapable of properly recognising and responding to that fullness of presence. Total fullness of presence to the Father and to the Son and so to one another which will be characteristic of the final kingdom does not, it would seem, belong in history, but it will eventually overcome the ambiguity of history as well as the disintegration and separation of death.

In the coming of that fullness of presence and power, God will reveal himself as he really is, which in New Testament terms is conceived as dynamic creative love. The fragmentary experience of being loved and loving which characterises our historical lives will meet its source and fulfilment in the God who is love.

The loving creativity or creative love of God which has been expressed in our uniqueness as individual persons, and in our unity as his family or community, provides the dynamism for growing differentiation in unity through history to the point where it transcends history by meeting the incoming, attracting God of the final kingdom.[12]

Kingdom and freedom

It is the same creating and attracting God that challenges and enables us to integrate our biological, psychological and social dimensions into a self-possession and self-disposition which even here and now may be described as the freedom of the sons/daughters of God. It is the freedom which transformed, however haltingly in history, tribe into community. It is that history which provides the basis for transforming history itself. The transformation already begun by the kingdom realising itself may be discerned by persons and communities becoming the subjects of their history, sharing the power and presence of the ultimate subject of history. Here we are, to adopt a phrase of Liberation Theology, concerned with salvation of history rather than with the history of salvation. The completion of that salvation of history and of its subjectivisation breaks out of history in response to the coming God in his final kingdom.

Kingdom and conversion

The 'already' and 'not yet', the present power and the future attraction, provide the dynamism for the Christian understanding of the future-oriented course of mankind, personally and socially. Critical moments in that course deserve a little more attention.

The record of Jesus' original preaching linked the announcement of the kingdom with the call to conversion, repentance, return, metanoia. The significance of conversion in human openness and reception of the inbreaking kingdom requires much fuller treatment than is possible here. Let me review briefly a few factors relevant to our purposes.

The turn or return to the inbreaking God is a disjunction or discontinuity with the previous life of sin and captivity. Man's creative receptivity in face of this divine initiative leads to new life and liberty after the death and slavery of sin. The conversion response is of course a return of love for love out of our condition of sin. That return in love to the Father involves a return in love to the neighbour as the New Testament clearly teaches – both in its understanding of the two great commandments and in its unique linking of one's forgiveness by the Father with one's forgiveness of and reconciliation with the neighbour. Conversion, like love, relates men to other men as well as to the Father God. It has in that sense a clearly social dimension.

Is there a further social dimension? Is the call to repentance possible for, and demanded of, societies and groups as well as individuals? The immediate New Testament evidence does not so clearly emphasise this but the overall thrust of God's dealings with mankind, Israel and the new community of the Saints suggests that, as the relationship between God and mankind has an inescapably social character which in turn applies to the approaching rule or kingdom of God, the summons to repentance as a way of entry to the kingdom applies also to societies and groups. We have still a long way to go in our theological understanding as well as in our sacramental and ritual expression before that insight becomes an effective part of Christian consciousness and praxis. Yet without it I am not sure that a fruitful connection can be made between the ethics of social development and theology of the kingdom of God.

At the more confined ecclesial level I would see the 'sacramental' expression of social conversion as the opportunity for the divided churches to acknowledge the sinfulness of their divisions in face of their one God, to disown these divisions before that God, to turn in genuine Christian concern to one another. Without such continuous conversion growth in unity is impossible. As conversion takes greater hold on us as Christian communities intercommunion will be its necessary and normal expression. And not just the casual eucharistic hospitality of one Christian community for a member of another, important as that may be in itself, but the God-given flowering of the dynamic turning to one another of whole Christian communities which he has already initiated. The absence of the relationship now is a clear countersign to the proper role of the churches in the coming of the kingdom.

The cost of conversion

One further point on the conversion to the kingdom. Conversion is a costly process. The kingdom cannot be had on the cheap. The rich young man was daunted by the cost. The radical sayings of Jesus about hating father and mother and the kingdom parables of the Treasure in the Field or the Pearl of Great Price (Matthew 13, 44–5)[13] so emphasise the totality of the demand which became more concrete in the call to share not only the life of Jesus but also his death.

Taking up the cross after Jesus' fashion and at his call and dying with him to one's own self-enclosed sinful world are the marks of the true disciple, the genuine accepter of the kingdom. The kingdom most fully proclaimed in the Resurrection is reached by way of the crucifixion. This indicates at once the inevitable price to be paid in terms of suffering, of renunciation in self-giving and dying, and the definitive triumph over that suffering and dying promised in Resurrection. Such death and resurrection are partially realised as the kingdom is, in personal and social history. They illustrate the tragic and comic (I speak in classical terms) elements of life for the Christian whose hope in the promise does not permit his final despair at the tragic.

In attending to the shadow side of human and Christian loving in this way, we are reminded of the fragility and vulnerability of our personal and social attainments which may at any time be overcome by the selfish hostile forces at work in our personal and social structures. More deeply and paradoxically we recognise that our ambiguous personal and social structures are under the judgment of and challenge of the inbreaking kingdom and the disruption of its converting and transforming power. The extent of the provisionality of our situation at any time is only fully revealed in the light of the Christian understanding of God's kingdom.

Eschatology and social ethics

In earlier chapters and in the discussion of the kingdom some notice has been taken at least indirectly of the interaction between human society at different levels and the kingdom of God. Here I must attempt to draw together some important strands.

The future, eschatological discontinuous character of the kingdom based on God's activity and not on man's achievement, which was recovered by Weiss[14] and Schweitzer[15] at the turn of the century cannot now, I believe, be open to further dispute. But neither can the later recognition of, in Dodd's phrase,[16] the 'realised' dimension of the kingdom, or as Jeremias[17] more expressly puts it, the kingdom in process of realising itself. The tension between the 'already' and 'not yet' has to be supplemented by a tension between divine initiative and human response to provide a full theological understanding of the meaning and direction, validity and limitations of social ethics.[18]

These tensions cohere in an enriching way with some of the tensions already discussed within social ethics itself as expressed in its future orientation, and the inherent provisionality of all its achievements and the tension between the striven for and given by, which structures all human existence and activity. The historical dimension, with its thrust towards subjectivisation and threat by objectivisation even unto final historical tragedy, has been adequately outlined already. And differentiation in unity which society is called to promote may be interpreted as the human expression of God's creative loving and loving creation of mankind. The elements of personal and social conversion appropriate to entering the kingdom have their secular and ethical counterparts in the radical change of person and structures even unto revolution which societies sometimes require.

In summary it may be asserted that social ethics in its

true understanding and practice expresses, is challenged by and given final power and significance by the in-breaking presence and power of God we call the kingdom.

Church and kingdom

With a minor digression on inter-church conversion I have so far resolutely ignored what to many people is the proper locus of God's activity in the world, the church.

In the not very distant past, church and kingdom were frequently identified. Contemporary theology for the most part denies that identification, with good reason in scriptural text and theological tradition. Yet the role of the church remains critical in preserving and proclaiming the message of the kingdom, in mediating through its community life as expressed in word, sacrament and loving ministry the understanding, the witness and the power of the in-breaking kingdom. Only in reference to the community of the church, and its god-given resources and human responses, can we discern the full dimension of God's reign as it emerges throughout human society and human history.

Yet the church is not the kingdom. It is not even the complete earthly, historical form of the kingdom. It is a realisation and an instrument of the kingdom. In its link with the original Christian community and in its resources of word and sacrament derived from that community, it may be described as *the* instrument of that kingdom. But it is not the only one. And it is not a perfect one. Its human fallibility and failure are notorious. It continually stands under the judgment of the kingdom as manifested through the church's own resources of word and sacrament, prophecy and discernment, or through the wider manifestations and realisations of the kingdom discernible throughout human society and history. It might take the tragic divisions of a reformation, or the destructive hostility of a French revolution or the searing and scathing analysis of a Marx or a Freud to awaken the church from its self-absorption and self-glorification, its betrayal of its divine task for human prestige or security or power, and liberate it to become once again a genuine instrument of the kingdom.

The criteria of its fidelity to this mission should include the ethics of society as approached here. The church is a society of human beings, united in confessing Jesus as Lord; but that unity, the manner and justification of that confession as a community confession, must endorse and respect the dignity, equality, freedom and participation of the individual members in promoting unity in Christ through deeper differentiation.

One can at least doubt that the churches really recognise, accept and live this kind of ethics, not as a form of purely human achievement but as an expression of and response to the presence of the Lord which they claim and proclaim. In so far that they do not recognise, accept and live such an ethics, how far is their proclamation negated and their claim invalidated?

The easy answers are out. The easy 'yes, that their proclaiming and claiming are then to be rejected' reduces Christianity to ethics; divine presence and power to human virtue and achievement. The easy 'no, that their proclaiming and claiming are untouched' implies a total separation between the divine and human, faith and ethics, gospel and law, which is false to the wider

Christian tradition. The ambiguity of the church's position as instrument of the kingdom has to be continually recognised. The tension between its claims as particular locus of God's message and power and its own error and infidelity must be continually recognised, not in a spirit of cynicism or apathy, but in a spirit of surrender to judgment, acceptance of challenge and recognition in love of the continuous saving power of God.

The provisionality of the church, its structures and teaching, is called for by the over-riding claims of the kingdom which transcend the church in peoples, time and place. The church is indispensable in our present condition and God's present dispensation for mankind as a whole. That condition understood in the context of human weakness and divine power should lead to a modest yet persistent church, untiring in the search for self-conversion as it is in the promotion of conversion of outsiders to the God of Jesus Christ and to each other.

Church and political commitment

As such an instrument of God's kingdom the church operates within the wider society in the interests of the fuller understanding of the human, deeper differentiation in creative freedom, and the true communion of respected and participating equals. In all this it is exposed to the conflict-ridden, ambiguous character of society. It cannot avoid conflict except at the expense of endorsing the mighty against the weak. Conflict will then demand taking sides with the weak and exploited and oppressed after the example and teaching of Jesus and in accord with the basis and structure of social ethics.

In doing so the churches act as genuine moral agents and as agents of the kingdom. But they do so in the deeper knowledge of the provisionality of all political arrangements and their need for constant reform. The provisionality of results is inescapable but it does not make the call to commitment any less firm.

The church has a further responsibility. In supporting the weak and exploited it must keep open the way to reconciliation in justice, equality and freedom. The exploiter is no less called to the kingdom than the exploited. He is politically and socially no less in need of liberation from his admittedly more comfortable slavery. And he is usually as person or class more in need of genuine conversion to God and neighbour/enemy without which reconciliation is meaningless.

Without any infallible insight into appropriate political programmes and yet faced by the risks of historical choice, the church remains truly church in its commitment if it also helps maintain the sense of provisionality and provide the structures for conversion and reconciliation. In this way a social ethics for Christians becomes a fully social ethics in that it applies not just to individual members but to the Christian communities as communities, and proclaims thereby the deeper significance of injustice and exploitation, the limitations of the next necessary stage of liberation and the need for and possibility of reconciliation through conversion that may be politically expressed even in revolution. In adopting such a stance the church(es) will face a difficult and uncertain future but may be led to some of that understanding and liberation whereby the truth of Jesus Christ sets men free with the freedom of the

children of God, a freedom in communion with him and
with one another.

Notes

1 The literature is immense. Recent and helpful for my purposes:
   Schnackenburg, R., *God's Rule and Kingdom* (New York–London,
   1963); Perrin, N., *The Kingdom of God in the Teaching of Jesus*
   (London–Philadelphia, 1963); Perrin, N., *Jesus and the Language of
   the Kingdom* (London–Philadelphia, 1976); Pannenberg, W.,
   Theology and the Kingdom of God (ed. Neuhaus, R. J.) (Philadelphia,
   1969).
2 Compare Hopkins, C. Howard, *The Rise of the Social Gospel in
   American Protestantism* (New Haven, Conn., 1967).
3 Compare Grenholm, C. H., *Christian Social Ethics in a Revolutionary
   Age* (Uppsala, 1973).
4 See above: chapter 1, note 1.
5 Temple was a prolific writer on a wide range of topics. Among
   works relevant here are *The Kingdom of God* (London, 1912);
   Christianity and the Social Order (London, 1942); *Christianity and the
   State* (London, 1928); and his critical Gifford Lectures *Nature, Man
   and God* (London, 1934).
6 Compare Grenholm, *op. cit.* A valuable addition to the Bennett
   corpus which Grenholm could not include in his study is *The Radical
   Imperative: From Theology to Social Ethics* (Philadephia, 1975).
7 In an expanding literature Gutierrez, G., *A Theology of Liberation*
   (New York, 1973) may still be taken as a typical and even standard
   work. See below, note 8.
8 Primarily associated with Metz and Moltmann. Compare Metz, J.
   B., *Theology of the World* (London–New York, 1969). The works of
   Moltmann are very extensive. Central is his 'trilogy': *Theology of
   Hope, The Crucified God* and *The Church in the Power of the Spirit*.
      Both Liberation Theology and Political Theology reflect a
   growing dialogue with Marxism which at least implicitly is
   influential in all discussion of Kingdom of God and social ethics
   today. Compare Hebblethwaite, P., *The Christian–Marxist Dialogue
   and Beyond* (London, 1977) for a recent survey of the interchange. A
   useful selection of essays in interchange may be found in
   Oestreicher, P. (ed.), *The Christian–Marxist Dialogue* (London,
   1969).

Among the more valuable recent works which come to grips explicitly with Marxism in terms of political and liberation theology are: Bonino, J. M., *Christians and Marxists* (London, 1976); Fierro, A., *The Militant Gospel* (London–New York, 1977); Petulla, J., *Christian Political Theology, A Marxian Guide* (New York, 1972).

9 I have developed this more fully in 'New horizons of Christian marriage' in *Beyond Tolerance*, ed. Michael Hurley (London, 1975).

10 Compare McDonagh, E., 'Nationalism and the Christian'', chapter 8 in *Gift and Call*.

11 Schnackenburg, Perrin, *op. cit.*

12 Pannenberg, *op. cit.*

13 Crossan, J. D., *In Parables* (New York–London, 1973) sets the discussion of these two parables (pp. 34ff) in a much wider and richer context of direct relevance to us.

14 Weiss, J., *Jesus' Proclamation of the Kingdom of God* (London, 1971).

15 Schweitzer, A., *The Quest of the Historical Jesus* (London, 1954 (first edition 1910)).

16 Dodd, C. H., *The Parables of the Kingdom* (London, 1935).

17 Jeremias, J., *The Parables of Jesus* (London, 1954).

18 In all this I owe a great deal to the works of Perrin and Schnackenburg already cited.